FLIGHTS OF IMAGINATION

FLIGHTS

EXTRAORDINARY WRITING ABOUT BIRDS

of IMAGINATION

edited by **RICHARD CANNINGS**

GREYSTONE BOOKS
D&M PUBLISHERS INC.
Vancouver/Toronto/Berkeley

Greystone Books
An imprint of D&M Publishers Inc.
2323 Quebec Street, Suite 201
Vancouver BC Canada V5T 4S7
www.greystonebooks.com

Library and Archives Canada Cataloguing in Publication
Flights of imagination : extraordinary writing about birds /
Richard Cannings, editor.

ISBN 978-1-55365-535-0

1. Birds—Anecdotes. 2. Bird watching—Anecdotes.
1. Cannings, Richard J. (Richard James)

QL677.5.F54 2010   598   C2009-905390-X

Cover design by Heather Pringle
Text design by Naomi MacDougall
Printed and bound in Canada by Friesens
Printed on acid-free paper that is forest friendly (100% post-consumer
recycled paper) and has been processed chlorine-free
Distributed in the U.S. by Publishers Group West

We gratefully acknowledge the financial support of the Canada
Council for the Arts, the British Columbia Arts Council, the Province
of British Columbia through the Book Publishing Tax Credit, and
the Government of Canada through the Book Publishing Industry
Development Program (BPIDP) for our publishing activities.

Mixed Sources
Cert no. SW-COC-001271
© 1996 FSC
FSC

CONTENTS

INTRODUCTION

. . . .

(RICHARD CANNINGS)

BIRDS HAVE inspired storytellers since the dawn of civilization. From the Haida stories of Raven to the dove
bringing news of land to Noah, birds have—perhaps to a
greater extent than other living things—been humanity's
link to the natural world. Anyone who has taken an English
literature course is familiar with poems such as Shelley's "To
a Skylark," Keats' "Ode to a Nightingale," and Tennyson's
"The Eagle." And I somehow remember belting out "She's
Like the Swallow" in more than a few Newfoundland bars.

Birds are irresistible. They are like us in more ways
than most other animals are; the majority live in a daylight
world, talking to each other through complex sounds and
showing off colorful finery. We meet them daily and with a
little effort we can learn to identify them in much the same

manner as they identify themselves. Their captivating songs often become an integral part of the soundtrack of our lives.

Birds are understandable. It is difficult to imagine the world of a shrew-mole as it searches for earthworms by tapping the moonlit ground with its long, sensitive nose, or to sense the chemical urges of a salmon coursing through cold waters, following molecular gradients to find its natal stream. But when you see a raven doing barrel-rolls in the sky, you immediately think, "I wish I could do that!" and you know that raven is having a good time. And when you hear a meadowlark singing loudly atop a sagebrush on a western morning, it is certainly tempting to believe that it enjoys being alive as much as you do. Some of this empathy may well be anthropomorphic, but it is a force that draws us into the natural world, or perhaps more accurately, out of our narrow human world and into the broader universe.

Birds can fly. This ability alone has propelled birds into the myths and minds of people for millennia. They come and go seemingly at will, their global wanderings firing our imaginations. It is not surprising that much of the writing about birds focuses on migration, a stirring reminder of the annual cycle and the cycle of life itself.

Wherever you go in the world, there are birds—albatrosses wheeling over the deepest oceans, penguins sliding on Antarctic ice, roadrunners dashing across desert sands, flocks of geese migrating high over the Himalayas. And wherever there are birds, there are people watching them. Some people simply enjoy watching birds at backyard feeders and may not feel the need to identify their species. Others fall under a more serious spell.

I didn't have any choice in the matter—my parents were naturalists and we were out watching birds at every opportunity. I was out on Christmas Bird Counts when I was six years old and started keeping track of all the birds I saw when I was nine. My father taught me how to call in pygmy owls like other fathers teach their sons how to fish. So it's not surprising that I often find myself looking at the world from a bird's point of view—when I drive by lush hayfields I think of bobolinks, not beef.

Many young birders grew up in families completely detached from nature and seem to have caught the birding bug from thin air. Kenn Kaufman was so enthralled with birds as a boy that he welcomed his family's move to Kansas because it would bring more western birds into his life. He quit school at age sixteen and hitchhiked around North America for several years in a quest to see as many birds as possible and learn all he could about birding. I'm not sure what his parents thought about his wanderings at that time, but he followed his passion and has become one of the best-known field guide authors in North America.

For others, a chance encounter with a single bird triggers the obsession. The sight of brilliant plumage on a tanager is enough to drive someone to a field guide that's been gathering dust on a shelf. Sometimes a more mundane-looking bird sets the process in motion. After a full year of living in Australia—a land dominated by large, colorful parrots—two friends of mine saw a small, brown bird in their garden. Later that day, they came across a field guide in a local book store and bought it to identify their tiny visitor as a scrubwren, probably the plainest bird on the continent. That discovery led them into a life of serious birding. For Steve Braunias it was simply a gull flying ghost-like past his balcony, sailing through the night streets of Auckland.

Birds act as a gateway drug into the more obscure recesses of natural history, into dragonfly territorial behavior, the molecular physiology of grasses, and, for some, even the chemical systematics of lichens. Birds open our eyes to the fact that the natural world and the human world are not separate but one and the same. When people start watching birds, they notice changes that they otherwise would have missed. As David Gessner notes in "Learning to Surf," it's good to get to know your neighbors.

Even observant naturalists may not realize that insect populations in their neighborhoods have dropped in recent decades as housing developments have replaced farmlands, but they do notice that the Barn Swallows have disappeared. Over the past thirty years I have been called innumerable times by birders worrying about the lack of one species or another, much as Richard Mabey worries in "The Naming of Parts." For a while I put it down to imperfect memories, but increasingly I realize that these birders are detecting a real downward spiral in the populations of many bird species.

And that knowledge reveals to us the impacts that our civilization is having on the biosphere that nurtures us, birds, and all living things. Rachel Carson wrote *Silent Spring* in 1962 to alert the world to the insidious and widespread effects of DDT and other pesticides. In choosing the title, she didn't emphasize the billions of fish that were being poisoned or the build up of contaminants in whale blubber—she pointedly used our love of birds as a succinct two-word warning.

Knowledge leads to concern, and concern should lead to action. Although Rachel Carson essentially kick-started the environmental movement with *Silent Spring,* many commentators point to Roger Tory Peterson's *A Field Guide to the Birds* as a necessary precursor. *Silent Spring* may well have gone unnoticed in an urbanized North American population disconnected with birds.

Concern for the plight of birds, and indeed of the planet as a whole, is a recurring theme in most of the pieces in this collection. And the picture is often not pleasant. The number of cranes wintering at Tram Chim, the setting of Susan Brownmiller's "Flying to Vietnam," has dropped significantly in recent years, the consequence of being a small refuge in a landscape increasingly altered by intensive farming and other changes. And Trevor Herriot's thoughts in "The Sparrow's Fall" are an eloquent reminder that, lately, each spring is more silent than the last. The birds are telling us that we must change our ways before it is too late. If we fail, the consequences may be more drastic for us than for the birds.

BEGINNINGS

SUMMER

. . . .

(STEVE BRAUNIAS)

I‍T WAS our first summer together. We had gone on a road trip up North over Christmas—five motels in seven nights, wet towels drying on the back seat. It was barbecue weather, New Zealand with sand in its hair, barefoot on hot pavements, undressed and dazed and unshaved, on vacation, gone fishing, fed and watered, half asleep, on good terms with itself, happy, setting off fireworks to see in the New Year.

There was an afternoon watching something spectacular—on the beach at Ruakaka, where a flock of gannets smashed into the water and came back up with fish. That was such a dazzling sight, but every day was dazzling. When I think about that week, I remember the sun high in the sky, the car strolling along on dusty roads between quiet fields of yellow short-haired grass. In the towns, fat kids stuffed themselves with ice-blocks and fizz outside dairies, and light breezes whisked dust down the middle of the street. The towns gave way to lines of gumtrees peeling in the sun. You could go hours without hearing a sound in our lazy sensual isles at the end of the world.

I was in love with New Zealand and in love with Emily. Summer with Emily—that's mainly what I remember. Emily swimming, Emily sleeping, Emily driving her passenger.

We went back to work. I don't remember much about that. Life was with Emily at my rented apartment near a bay, with Emily at her rented apartment in the city. Late one night, I stepped out on to her balcony for a cigarette. It was towards the end of January. A summer's evening, long past dark, the air finally cooling and only as warm as toast after the fructifying heat of daylight hours. I stood and smoked, and then a bird flew past right in front of my snoot. You could say it was any old bird—it was that common, unloved scavenger, a black-backed gull, a big quiet thing, in no apparent hurry, slowly flying past, then slowly circling back again, and its silent, sudden appearance in darkness was stranger than anything happening down below among the traffic and the street lights.

It felt like a jolt. The gull had come by so close; in the darkness its white body had glowed like a lamp swinging on a porch. No doubt it had good reason to be going about its business on an obscure hour in the middle of downtown Auckland. What business? Back then, I would have thought that God only knew, and it turned out that I was right— God had known, in an earlier summer, 1968–69 to be precise, when the roof-nesting habits of black-backed gulls in downtown Auckland were studied by Graham Turbott, a lovely man who at 92 is the godfather of New Zealand ornithology.

Turbott's report on the gulls, published in a 1969 issue of *Notornis,* referred to the observation of four pairs of birds at breeding sites around the city. Two chicks were hatched from a bulky nest of grass and paper on the roof of the Old Oxford Theatre on Queen Street; one chick hatched but died on the roof of a hot-water tank on top of the Chief Post Office. Chicks were seen to depart the nest in mid-January from the roof of the Magistrate's Court in Kitchener Street. At 24 Cook Street, according to a Miss J. Walker who "kept a constant watch" on the gulls' nest in the gutter at the edge of the roof, a young bird, fully fledged at six weeks, left with both its parents on February 7; it had hatched from its manger in the gutter on Christmas Day.

The bird I saw was an adult, and probably still feeding its chick. Black-backed gulls—*Larus dominicianus*—nest in large colonies of up to several thousand pairs in the greater outdoors of the coast, but form solitary two-parent families in the city. They can swallow a cutlet of mutton whole. Offal is also acceptable.

The oldest recorded New Zealand black-back was a been-there, ate-that 28 years old. In its adult prime, the bird isn't a bad looker; it has yellow eyes and a bright red smear on its bill. But it takes two molts and nearly three years before juveniles assume the smooth whiteness that glows like a lamp. Young black-backs are among the most unpleasant things on wings. A lot of people mistake these large mottled brutes for some other kind of bird, and refuse to throw them scraps, out of distaste for their appearance. No one should be in the least surprised that these plug-ugly thugs don't get any sex until they are at least four years old.

I didn't know any of these things when I saw the black-back brush past my nose that summer's evening. I didn't know nothing about any birds. But when I caught sight of that one bird, felt the jolt it gave, that white flash in the black night, I was bowled over with happiness, and I thought: birds, everywhere. Summer in New Zealand fills with so much light that we become the land of the long white page. Every corner, every margin is filled with birds.

As a weekly magazine columnist since 1999, a lot of my writing has imagined different kinds of maps of New Zealand—of the things and pleasures that are right in front of us, that tell almost a secret history of the place, that maybe even reveal an emotional truth about the place. And so I've written a series of columns about hot springs. About steak. About mangroves. About tearooms. About things and pleasures you can find all across the country, from one town or shore to the next, forming a grid. I now wanted very much to write about birds.

Birds of the city and town, on lawn and roof. Birds of the bush and the shore and the wide open sea. Paddock, lakeside, riverbank, wharf, telephone wire, bridge, swamp, alp: everywhere, birds. Migrants, most dramatically the bar-tailed godwit, flying for seven, eight days from Alaska without rest, until landfall in New Zealand. Common or garden varieties, like the blackbird and the house sparrow, brought to New Zealand by England's homesick colonists. Native endemics, some still around—the tui, the takahe—and some wiped out, extinct, ghosts of another time—the huia, the moa. Birds that have come and gone and may come again, such as the red-necked avocet, quite possibly the most amazing bird to ever grace these shores, but seldom straying here from its breeding grounds across the ditch in Brisbane. Birds nesting under bridges; birds nesting in sand. Big fat birds, birds as small as full stops, as a row of dots...

Could you be a bit more specific? Yes, in time. 2006 became my year of birds. I took down names. I saw birds I never knew existed. I became fascinated with birds that no longer existed, and with the literature of birds, with the social history of watching birds in New Zealand. I learned things. I shared pleasures. I saw another New Zealand, a particular geography where its borders and centers were defined by birds—a feathered New Zealand. And I saw another kind of New Zealander, their lives transformed, consumed, by birds.

I loved seeing what they had seen, that year, and years before. I loved discovering a simple truth: to watch a bird is to see the world in a completely different way.

I watched the birds—"Beside us," as poet Matthew Arnold wrote, "but alone"—and I watched the watchers. I watched the world of New Zealand with refreshed eyes. It was a great privilege. I felt alert, awed, alive. And it was strange timing the way that marvelous year coincided with something else in my life, something amazing, that happened along the way.

NOT QUITE *the* WEST

. . . .

(KENN KAUFMAN)

I WENT OUT on the road, to chase my dream, at the age of
nine.

That was what I used to tell the girls I met while I was
bumming rides around North America in the 1970s; and,
of course, they didn't believe me any more than you do.
But the truth is that the seeds for all my later travels were
planted on my ninth birthday. That was the day the family
moved, the day the last thing was packed and we drove away
from the house in Indiana for the last time.

That day's drive still comes to mind with surprising clarity: the tree-lined streets of South Bend falling away behind
us, the country opening up, the Illinois state line coming
up as a milestone to be remarked upon. My father pointing
things out and explaining things: the construction of the

bridges, the uses of the farm machinery, the history behind the "Land of Lincoln" signs. My mother, so good with words, making up little poems and word games to amuse the kids in the back seat.

Always the quiet and introverted one, I was quieter than usual that day, sitting in the back and staring out the window. My parents noticed and said once again they were sorry we had had to move on my birthday. But they need not have worried. Already a rebel in the quietest way, I had decided for myself that holidays or special days meant nothing if they were dictated by the calendar. Any day might be a special one—you just had to get outside and see if it was.

This was an incredibly special day because of where we were: out on the highway, with the tires drumming hypnotically on the pavement, and with new possibilities everywhere just beyond the wide horizon. That day I was first aware of feeling a significant difference from my parents and my brothers. They were thinking about our destination, mostly, or about the place we were leaving behind. I was focused on the road itself, on the feeling of going somewhere, anywhere, just going. As the sun moved down the western sky directly ahead of us, it seemed to draw us along. A crazy sense came over me that we should just follow the sun and keep pace with it, around and around the earth, and the day would never end.

And as long as the day was unending I would be staring out the car windows with all the intensity of a nine-year-old boy, scanning the fences, the wires, the open fields, the distant treetops, and the sky, because I had a purpose, a mission, a passion: I was watching for birds.

A CURIOSITY about nature—or about picture books on nature—had come to me out of nowhere in earliest childhood. By the time I was six, having concluded that there were no tigers or comets or dinosaurs in our humdrum Indiana neighborhood, I had turned to birds as the best thing available. After that I had never looked back. My interest became a driving force, fueled by books from the local branch library, encouraged by parents who promoted any genuine learning and so had refused for years to have a television in the house.

The other boys in my neighborhood idolized baseball players or movie cowboys, but my hero was the great bird expert, Roger Tory Peterson. I had checked his books out from the library and read them over and over again. I had studied all of his paintings, especially of the birds I could not find in the South Bend suburbs. When my parents started to talk about moving, my first thought was "New birds!"

Poring over Peterson's bird guides every night, I had figured out something that seemed important: every bird had its place. None was "free as a bird." A few kinds were found all over the continent, but they were the exceptions. Many birds were regional, found only in the South, for example, or only in the West. Some were limited to only a few small areas. Still others were rare visitors to North America. But no two species seemed to have quite the same range on the map, and no two places had quite the same birdlife. It followed that the way to see more kinds of birds was to go to more different places.

So when my father started casting around for employment possibilities in other states, I pestered him constantly for the latest news on the job front. Every time a new place was mentioned, I would look up everything I could find about the birding potential there.

There was brief discussion of a job in Seattle. I read about ancient mossy forests along the fog-shrouded coast, and about little seabirds called auklets and murrelets on the waters of Puget Sound. Then my parents also read some things about the area, and rainy Seattle was out: they were looking for a warm, *dry* climate. The job search, and my basic bird research, shifted to locales that were farther south and farther inland.

A job in Utah was considered, and I read about Sage Grouse strutting on sagebrush flats, and about flocks of shorebirds in the marshes of Bear River. Possibilities in California came up, and I read about sickle-billed California Thrashers skulking in the chaparral, and about the last of the California Condors sailing over wilderness crags. New Mexico held some promise for a while, and I read about Roadrunners dueling with rattlesnakes in the cactus gardens, about Western Tanagers flashing through the mountain pine forests like burnt gold, and about Prairie Falcons keeping lonely vigils on the plains.

Because they wanted a dry climate, my parents never really looked at anything in the eastern states—so my early reading focused on birds of the West. Years later I would realize that the East had some of the best birding on the continent; but as a bird-crazed kid of eight years old I was convinced that the West was the place to be.

And then the best job offer came from Wichita, Kansas. Farther west than Indiana, Kansas was not far enough over to have birdlife typical of the West. But that was where we moved.

AT FIRST the birds of suburban Kansas seemed pretty similar to those of suburban Indiana: mostly sparrows and starlings. But spring was coming, so I thought things might improve.

They did. One day when I was walking home from school I saw a bird the size of a robin, but patterned in pale yellow and gray, perched on a wire near my house. Running home, I grabbed my field guide (stubbornly, I used Peterson's *western* bird guide, even though Wichita was in the region covered by the eastern book) and rushed back to find the bird still there. Squinting first at the bird and then at the field guide pictures, I figured out what it was: a Western Kingbird. *Western* Kingbird! I was ecstatic. Maybe I was in the West after all. In that instant, the Western Kingbird became my favorite bird.

More kingbirds arrived over the following weeks. There were few large trees in our neighborhood, but the kingbirds built their nests against the crossarms of telephone poles and perched on the wires to survey the surroundings. They seemed utterly fearless. If a larger bird, such as a crow or a kestrel, came anywhere near their nest, the kingbirds would dart out at once with staccato sputtering cries, harassing or even attacking the bigger bird to drive it away.

During that summer and the next, I found many kingbird nests. I spent hours watching them and taking notes. I admired the aggressive exploits of the adult birds as they drove away predators or rivals, tried to see what kinds of insects they brought to feed their young, and watched the actions of the young birds when they left the nest and learned to fly.

I was not allowed too far from the nest myself then, so I couldn't find very many different kinds of birds. Those I did find, I spent a lot of time on: watching, drawing sketches, taking notes. But gradually I ranged farther afield, on foot and by bicycle. As I found more kinds of birds, and as I entered my teens, a new restlessness took over.

It began with knowing my birds well enough to know them at a distance: a Western Kingbird on a distant wire, a Lark Sparrow calling its metallic *chip* as it flew overhead, an Orchard Oriole singing its jumble of notes a block away. Soon I could predict where I would see them: the Warbling Vireos would be in willows along the canal, the Swainson's Hawks would be sailing over fields along Meridian Avenue, the Solitary Sandpipers would be lurking along the bank downriver from Herman Hill. With a little planning, I could head out on my bike and see dozens of birds in one day—and the more I saw, the more I wanted to see.

One day I saw fifty different species, and I thought that was an unbeatable record for my little area; but then I hit sixty, and then seventy-five. Finally—at the height of spring migration, when flocks were passing through on their way north—I was able to break one hundred in a day.

For a lone kid on a bike in Kansas to see and hear a hundred kinds of birds in one day was, I felt, a real accomplishment. Even though it was just a game, it was a game based on knowledge; and the more I knew, the more I wanted to learn.

And the more I learned, the more I became dissatisfied with just seeing the birds in my neighborhood. I knew that North America had more than seven hundred species of birds, and I knew I could spend a lifetime birding in Kansas and not see more than half of them. Every bird had its place. If I wanted to see Snail Kites or Green Kingfishers or

Painted Redstarts, I would have to go to where they lived. They were never going to come to me.

State law dictated that I had to stay in school until I was sixteen. As my sixteenth birthday approached, I began to dream of how much I could learn about birds by leaving school as soon as it was legal and heading out of the state. The fact that I would miss two and a half years of high school didn't bother me.

But it bothered some people. I made the mistake of mentioning my idea, offhandedly, to one of my teachers, and the next thing I knew I was in the school counselor's office.

"Why is this a big deal?" I wanted to know. "Tommy Wells dropped out a couple of months ago, and nobody said a word."

"Wells?" The counselor frowned. "Your friend Mr. Wells was not really applying himself to his studies or his grades. Now, your situation is different."

"I didn't say he was my friend. I hardly knew him. But did anyone try to keep him from dropping out?" "Think about how that sounds," said the counselor. "Think about the word 'dropout.' Giving up. Dropping out. Do you want to be a loser? I've looked at your record with your grades, and your honors classes, you'd have no trouble getting into college. And the student council at Truesdell last year— wouldn't you be ashamed of yourself if you went from student council president to dropout?"

"So you're saying Tommy didn't have good grades, so it's okay to let him drop out. That's backwards. If his grades were bad, maybe he needs a diploma more than I do."

"He was failing school."

"Or school was failing him," I shot back, and then was sorry I had said it. "Have you really looked at my record? I was the first student council prez to get kicked out of class for causing trouble. I was only elected because the rebels voted for me. Look, uh, Sir, I don't cause trouble when I'm studying things I want to learn. But I'm wasting my time in these classes."

By now he was angry and perplexed. "Do you want to waste your life instead? If you want to do anything in life, you have to at least finish high school! You're no different from everyone else!"

My silent response was: Listen, Jack, *everyone* is different from everyone else, and we ought to be celebrating that instead of squashing it. But out loud I just said that I was bored and needed more challenge. They bent the rules to put me into what was usually a senior honors class. There I flirted with the older girls, argued about literature with everyone, and got an A in the course. When the semester was over, I left school.

During June and July of that year—1970, the year I turned sixteen—I worked as the nature instructor at a summer camp. In August, with money saved from that job, I hit the road.

There was a day at the end of August that held a special symbolism for me. Not that I did anything unusual that day: like the days before and after, I spent it looking at birds. That day was significant because I knew that, back at home, kids my age were going back to school.

They had the clang of locker doors in the halls of South High in Wichita, Kansas. I had a nameless mountainside in Arizona, with sunlight streaming down among the pines, and Mexican songbirds moving through the high branches. My former classmates were moving toward their education, no doubt, just as I was moving toward mine, but now I was traveling a road that no one had charted out for me...and my adventure was beginning.

WESTERN MEADOWLARK

. . . .

(RICHARD CANNINGS)

MY EARLIEST memories are of meadowlarks. Their songs rang through my open bedroom window as the morning sky brightened, and they have become etched in my mind as a coordinate of home. Whereas the hypnotic sounds of crickets and lisping sprinklers were my lullabies as a very young boy, meadowlarks were my alarm clocks, waking me to the warm summer mornings. Their songs are the anthem of the grasslands, as much a part of life in the West as the taste of saskatoon berries, the smell of sagebrush after a thunderstorm, and the color of the evening sky above the black mountains in the summer twilight.

Just before I was born, my parents built a house in a new rural subdivision carved out of wild bunchgrass. Before our family owned the land it was meadowlark country, and for the first five or six years that we lived there the birds came back to the yard each spring, until the young apple orchard turned the prairie into a deciduous woodland and they had to look elsewhere to nest. Western meadowlarks are birds of the grasslands and cannot tolerate forests, though they will happily sing from a ponderosa pine growing high and lonesome amid the grass. But for those few years the meadowlarks were a big part of my backyard, the males singing from the freshly planted apple trees, the young riding on the back of the tractor as it mowed the long grass in midsummer.

My brothers and I spent much of our childhood "across the fence," playing on the unplowed grasslands of the Penticton Indian Reserve. In winter we would toboggan down the steep slopes of the hills, using the snowdrifts behind each sagebrush as jumps. When spring came we looked for the first buttercup, then, when the ground was yellow with them, tried to find the one with the most petals. I learned which plants were tastiest and was particularly fond of the tangy flavor of a distinctive gray, grass-like leaf that came directly out of the spring soil. Only later did I learn to my embarrassment that I had been desecrating one of the most beautiful plants of the grassland, the mariposa lily. We would push toy trucks around the clumps of prickly pear cactus, hide in the rose thickets, and try—always unsuccessfully—to sneak up on coyotes. Occasionally we would see more uncommon birds—a flock of gray partridge exploding from the shrubs, a burrowing owl standing watchfully next to its subterranean nest, or a long-billed curlew calling mournfully in the distance—but we were always surrounded by meadowlarks. Their songs were the soundtrack of our young lives.

Loud and melodic, meadowlark songs sail through the dry air, advertising the presence of a male with a territory.

One might think that meadowlarks and other grassland songbirds are at a disadvantage when compared with forest birds in that they don't have any high trees from which to broadcast their songs far and wide. But the wide open spaces are an advantage for being both seen and heard—there are no trees to get in the way. To get a high singing site, many grassland birds—the sky lark is a famous example—simply fly up into the air, giving long songs while they are mere specks against the blue sky. Male meadowlarks have a flight song, but it is not as musical (to the human ear) as the song they give while standing on fence posts or other perches.

Their beautiful songs probably gave meadowlarks their name, but they are not related to other larks. The lark family is more or less confined to the Old World—Eurasia and Africa—with only one representative in North America, the horned lark. Meadowlarks are members of the family Icteridae, a large and diverse group of New World birds that includes the blackbirds and orioles. Again, neither is related to their Old World namesakes.

To add visual impact to their songs, many grassland birds have striking plumage patterns that are visible only from below. Most birds (indeed, most animals) have a characteristic dark-above-light-below color pattern that is clearly advantageous when they want to blend in with either the dark ground when seen from above or the pale sky when seen from below. A meadow-dwelling cousin of the meadowlark, the bobolink, has a display plumage that is the complete opposite of this normal pattern: the males are jet black below and mostly white above, making them easily visible while they chatter out the song for which they are named. Meadowlarks are almost invisible from above;

their pale brown plumage speckled with black and white is indistinguishable from the dry grass they hide in. But seen from below they are a sight to behold—eye-popping yellow breasts set off with a bold black v necklace and bright white outer tail feathers that flash against the sky.

Not coincidentally, the meadowlark plumage pattern is roughly repeated in the horned lark, which shares many North American grasslands with meadowlarks. There is a group of birds in African grasslands, the longclaws, which look even more like meadowlarks—the color patterns are essentially identical, and only a more slender body form and longer hind claw set the longclaws apart. The longclaws, members of the pipit family, have orange- and red-breasted species as well—a pattern repeated in several meadowlark species found in South American grasslands. The meadowlarks and longclaws are a textbook example of convergent evolution. They are totally unrelated species that have evolved very similar plumages in response to similar evolutionary forces—in this case the need to be seen and recognized while performing courtship flight songs in wide-open spaces.

Most grassland birds nest directly on the ground for obvious reasons—there are few bushes or trees in sight. A meadowlark nest is tucked deep into a hollow beside a clump of grass, hidden completely by dried grass that bends over the nest and its entrance. The female sits so tightly on the nest that few are ever found; I have seen only two in my life despite many days of searching. The nests I have found were discovered accidentally when I literally stepped on the incubating females, causing them to explode away on those short meadowlark wings. Luckily I didn't damage the nest contents. Because predators such as skunks and coyotes would love to find the nestlings, the adults are very wary of approaching the nest when feeding their young. If you ever try to find a meadowlark nest by watching an adult with a beak full of grasshoppers, you will find yourself in a long waiting game, the bird patiently giving warning calls to its mate, knowing you will soon tire of the game and go away.

A more unfortunate characteristic that almost all grass-land species in North America share is declining populations. Once each year I get up very early on a June morning and do a Breeding Bird Survey along a standard 25-mile-long (40-kilometer) route in the Okanagan Valley. I leave home about 3:45 AM and drive through the dark to the starting point, getting my data sheets ready under cold, clear skies while listening to the first birds of the day—robins, blue-birds, juncos. Up on the hill, a poorwill gives one last series of calls before going to sleep for the day. I have to begin the survey at exactly 4:20 AM, listen for three minutes at the first stop, noting what I see and hear, then drive a half-mile (nearly a kilometer) to the next stop, and repeat the procedure. The survey takes more than four hours to complete, and by the fiftieth and final stop I am certainly ready for either a strong coffee or a nap. It takes a lot of motivation to get out of bed and get the survey done each year, but the results are well worth the effort—a long-term data set that tells biologists more about bird population trends than any other program in North America.

When I began this survey in 1973 I used to count about fifty meadowlarks along my route—they were the com-monest species on my list. For the past six years I've only heard about twenty each time, and robins have replaced them at the top of the list. Data from almost three hundred similar surveys from across western Canada show the same result—there are only about half the number of western meadowlarks now that there were thirty years ago. Other grassland birds—sharp-tailed and sage grouse, ferruginous hawks, burrowing owls, horned larks, Sprague's pipits, and longspurs—have declined to equal or greater degrees. In fact, as a group, grassland birds are declining faster than the birds associated with any other habitat in North America. What is it about grasslands?

Perhaps the simplest explanation is that grasslands are easy targets for development. There are no trees to cut down, no swamps to drain—just flatten the land out a bit and build the houses, as my parents did fifty years ago. But it is agriculture, not urban development, that is the biggest threat to grasslands. Across most of the West, all farmers have to do is plow the fertile soil, plant their crops, and pray for rain. Over the last century, water diversions have provided ample irrigation for the development of dry grasslands, saving the need for prayer in many areas. The statistics are clear-cut: 99 percent of the moister grasslands of the West, the tall-grass prairies, are gone forever, and about 70 percent of drier grasslands have disappeared as well. The latter are suffering another onslaught—that of invasive weeds that have taken over much of the bunchgrass hills of the West. When I walk across some of the pockets of grass left in southern British Columbia I'm often hard-pressed to see any native plants other than scattered sagebrush and rabbitbrush—the rest is Dalmatian toadflax, diffuse knapweed, sulfur cinquefoil, and cheatgrass.

Meadowlarks are highly migratory in the northern part of their range; in October I often kick up a small flock in the golden grass as they gather for the flight south. The habitat loss that Canadian meadowlarks suffer may be exacerbated while they are wintering in the southwestern United States or northern Mexico. Those reaching Arizona may find condos where grass grew the previous year, and those headed for Texas and Mexico are often confronted with intensively cultivated crops such as cotton. While the ground is frozen in winter the Canadian grasslands are almost completely empty of birdlife. But as the spring sun melts the snow and the buttercups bloom, western meadowlarks are among the first birds to reclaim the awakening land. With the warmth in the air, the flashes of yellow, and the clear notes of meadowlark song, hope returns to the West.

LEARNING *to* SURF

. . . .

(DAVID GESSNER)

Out just beyond the breaking waves they sit there bobbing, two groups of animals, avian and human, pelicans and surfers. As they rise and fall on humps of water, the pelicans look entirely unperturbed, their foot-long bills pulled like blades into scabbards, fitting like puzzle pieces into the curves of their throats. The surfers, mostly kids, look equally casual. A girl lies supine on her board, looking up at the sky, one leg crossed over the other in an almost exaggerated posture of relaxation. For the most part the birds and surfers ignore each other, rising up and dropping down together as the whole ocean heaves and then sighs.

Pelicans are particularly buoyant birds and they bob high on the water as the surfers paddle and shift in anticipation. There is no mistaking that this is the relatively tense calm of before, rest before exertion. Soon the waves pick up and the kids paddle furiously, gaining enough speed to pop up and ride the crests of breaking surf. They glide in toward the beach where I stand, the better ones carving the water and ducking under and cutting back up through the waves.

I just recently moved to this southern island town, but I have been here long enough to know that those who pursue this sport are guided by a kind of laid-back monomania. Each morning I bring my four-month-old daughter down to the local coffee shop, and each morning the talk is of one thing. The ocean, I've learned, is always referred to as it.

"What did it look like this morning?" one surfer asked another a few mornings back.

"Sloppy."

Remembering my own early-morning glance at the water I could understand what he meant, the way a series of waves came from the northwest, while another group muscled up from the south, and how the two collided and kicked up. Aesthetically it was beautiful, but practically, at least from a surfer's point of view, it made for a landscape of chop—not much to get excited about.

Another morning I heard this:

"How does it look today, dude?"

"Small."

"Nothing?"

"You can go out there if you want to build your morale."

It's easy enough to laugh at these kids, but I like the physical nature of their obsession, the way their lives center on being strong animals. In *When Elephants Weep,* Jeffrey Masson speculates that animals feel *funktionslust,* a German word meaning "pleasure taken in what one can do best." The strongest of the surfers, the ones who have grown up on the waves, must certainly feel this animal pleasure as they glide over and weave through the water.

I watch the surfers for a while longer, but when the pelicans lift off, I turn my focus toward their even more impressive athletic feats. Pelicans are huge and heavy birds, and the initial liftoff, as they turn into the wind and flap hard, is awkward. But once in the air they are all grace. They pull in their feet like landing gear and glide low between the troughs of the waves, then lift up to look for fish, flapping several times before coasting. If you watch them enough, a rhythm reveals itself: effort, *glide*, effort, *glide*. They are looking for small fish—menhaden or mullet most likely—and when they find what they are searching for they gauge the depth of the fish, and therefore the necessary height of the dive, a gauging guided by both instinct and experience. Then they pause, lift, measure again, and finally, plunge. The birds bank and twist and plummet, following their divining-rod bills toward the water. A few of them even turn in the air in a way that gives the impression they are showing off. If they were awkward in takeoff, now they are glorious.

There is something symphonic about the way the group hits the water, one bird after another: *thwuck, thwuck, thwuck*. At the last second before contact they become feathery arrows, thrusting their legs and wings backward and flattening their gular pouches. They are not tidy like terns and show no concern for the Olympian aesthetics of a small splash, hitting the surface with what looks like something close to recklessness. As soon as they strike the water, instinct triggers the opening of the huge pouch, and it umbrellas out, usually capturing fish, plural. While still underwater they turn again, often 180 degrees, so that when they emerge they'll be facing into the wind for takeoff. And when they pop back up barely a second later, they almost instantly assume a sitting posture on the water, once again bobbing peacefully. It's a little like watching a man serve a tennis ball who then, after the follow-through, hops immediately into a La-Z-Boy.

THE PELICANS calm me, which is good. I have tried to maintain a relaxed attitude since moving to this island, but at times it's hard. I had vowed that I would stay forever on Cape Cod, my old home, but it was my writing about how much I loved the Cape that led to the offer of a teaching job in this overcrowded North Carolina resort town of outboard motors, condos, and southern accents. My wife, Nina, had just given birth to our daughter, Hadley, and the lure of health insurance and a steady paycheck was irresistible.

The truth is, the move has unsettled me: in coming to this new place I find myself, and my confidence, getting shaky. If I've behaved well publicly, in the privacy of our new apartment I've at times started to fall apart. As each day unfolds, I grow ever less sure of myself.

One of the things that disorients me is the heat. It's the kind of heat that makes you want to lie down and give up, to start to cry and throw out your arms in surrender. I've known brutal cold in my life, but cold has the advantage of invigoration, at least initially. Now I understand the logic behind siestas; every instinct tells you to crawl to a cool dank place and lie there and be still.

Lifting my daughter into our un-air-conditioned Honda Civic feels like sliding her into a kiln, so we are desperately trying to buy a new car. But today the Toyota guy calls with bad news. Our credit report has come back and our loan has been rejected.

"You have weak stability," he tells me, reading from the report.

I nod and consider the poetry of his words.

BUT THERE are other moments, moments when I sense that this may not be such a bad place to live. With summer ending, the parking lots have begun to empty. There are fewer beach walkers and more pelicans. Each morning I take long walks with Hadley, and have begun to take field notes on my daughter. I'm struck daily by her creatureliness, and the fact that this squirming little apelike animal, barely two feet high (half a meter), has somehow been allowed to live in the same house with us. Nothing cuts through my doubts about having moved here quite like this new ritual of walking with my daughter in a papooselike contraption on my chest. On good days we make it all the way to the south end of the island where we stare out at the channel.

Many things have caught me off guard about being a father, but the most startling thing has been the sheer animal pleasure. "Joy is the symptom by which right conduct is measured," wrote Joseph Wood Krutch of Thoreau. If that's true then my conduct these days must be excellent.

This morning we watch two immature, first-year pelicans fly right over the waves, belly to belly with their shadows. It's exhilarating the way they lift up together and sink down again, rollercoastering, their wings nicking the crests of the waves. Eight more adult birds skim right through the valley between the waves, gliding by the surfers, sweeping upward before plopping onto the water.

Feeling that it's only polite to get to know my new neighbors, I've begun to read about the birds. I've learned that the reason they fly through the troughs between the waves is to cut down on wind resistance, which means they, like the surfers they fly past, are unintentional physicists. When I first started watching pelicans I kept waiting to hear their calls, expecting a kind of loud *quack-quork,* like a cross between a raven and a duck. But my books confirm what I have already noticed, that adult pelicans go through their lives as near mutes. Whether perched atop a piling in classic silhouette or crossing bills with a mate or bobbing in the surf, they remain silent.

Another group of adult birds heads out to the west, toward the channel, as Hadley and I turn home. Before moving here I never knew that pelicans flew in formations. They are not quite as orderly as geese—their vs always slightly out of whack—and the sight of them is strange and startling to someone from the North. Each individual takes a turn at the head of the v, since the lead bird exerts the most effort and energy while the birds that follow draft the leader like bike racers. These platoons fly overhead at all hours of day, appearing so obviously prehistoric that it seems odd to me that people barely glance up, like ignoring a fleet of pterodactyls.

Yesterday I saw a bird point its great bill at the sky and then open its mouth until it seemed to almost invert its pouch. My reading informs me that these exercises are common, a way to stretch out the distensible gular pouch so that it maintains elasticity. Even more impressive, I learn that the pouch, when filled, can hold up to twenty-one pints (ten liters)—seventeen and a half pounds (eight kilograms)—of water.

"I have had a lifelong love affair with terns," wrote my friend from Cape Cod, John Hay, a writer whom I have always admired for his sense of rootedness. I've come to pelicans late and so can't have my own lifelong affair. But I am developing something of a crush.

I'M NOT a good watcher. Well, that's not exactly true. I'm a pretty good watcher. It's just that sooner or later I need to do more than watch. So today I am floating awkwardly on my neighbor Matt's surfboard, paddling with my legs in a frantic eggbeater motion, attempting this new sport in this new place while keeping one eye on the pelicans. Even though you can't bring your binoculars, it turns out that this is a great way to birdwatch. The pelicans fly close to my board, and for the first time I understand how enormous they are. I've read that they are fifty inches (1.27 meters) from bill to toe, and have six-and-a-half-foot (two-meter) wingspans, but these numbers don't convey the heft of their presence. One bird lands next to me and sits on the water, tucking its ancient bill into its throat. Up close its layered feathers look very unfeatherlike, more like strips of petrified wood. I watch it bob effortlessly in the choppy ocean. Most birds with webbed feet have three toes, but brown pelicans have four, and their webbing is especially thick. While this makes for awkward waddling on land, it also accounts for how comfortable the birds look in the water.

I'm not nearly as comfortable. Two days ago I spent an hour out here with Matt, and yesterday we came out again. Despite his patience and coaching, I never stood up on my board, in fact I never made more than the most spastic attempts. Today has been no better. The best things about surfing so far are watching the birds and the way my body feels afterward when I am scalding myself in our outdoor shower. So it is with some surprise that I find myself staring back with anticipation as a series of good waves roll in, and it is with something close to shock that I find myself suddenly, mysteriously, riding on top of that one perfect (in my case, very small) wave. Before I have time to think I realize that I am standing, actually standing up and surfing. The next second I am thrown into the waves and smashed about.

But that is enough to get a taste for it.

I HAVE now been practicing my new art for three days. The pelicans have been practicing theirs for thirty million years. It turns out that the reason they look prehistoric is simple: they are. Fossils indicate that something very close to the same bird we see today was among the very first birds to take flight. They were performing their rituals—diving, feeding, courting, mating, nesting—while the world froze and thawed, froze and thawed again, and while man, adaptable and relatively frenetic, came down from the trees and started messing with fire and farming and guns.

What struck me first about these curious-looking birds was the grace of their flight. Not so the early ornithologists. In 1922, Arthur Cleveland Bent wrote of their "grotesque and quiet dignity" and called them "silent, dignified and stupid birds." A contemporary of Bent's, Stanley Clisby Arthur, went even further, describing the pelicans' habits with something close to ridicule. Arthur writes of the pelicans' "lugubrious expressions" and "ponderous, elephantine tread" and "undemonstrative habits," and says of their mating rituals that "they are more befitting the solemnity of a funeral than the joyous display attending most nuptials." His final insult is calling their precious eggs "a lusterless white."

Even modern writers seem to feel the need to lay it on thick: as I read I make a list of words that includes "gawky," "awkward," "comical," "solemn," "reserved," and, simply, "ugly." It never occurred to me that pelicans were so preposterous, though I'll admit that recently, as I kayaked by a sandbar full of birds, I laughed while watching a pelican waddle though a crowd of terns, like Gulliver among the Lilliputians. But "ugly" seems just mean-spirited.

When not seeing pelicans as comic or grotesque, human beings often describe them as sedate and sagelike. Perhaps this springs from a dormant human need to see in animals the qualities we wish we had. Compared to our own harried, erratic lives, the lives of the pelicans appear consistent, reliable, even ritualistic, as befits a bird that has been doing what it's been doing for thirty million years. And compared to their deep consistent lives, my own feels constantly reinvented, improvised. But before I get too down on myself, I need to remember that that's the kind of animal I am, built for change, for adaptation. Long before we became dull practitioners of agriculture, human beings were nomads, wanderers, capable of surviving in dozens of different environments.

Though barely able to hold their heads up at birth and fed regurgitated food by their parents while in the nest, new-born pelicans fledge within three months. The one year olds I watch flying overhead are already almost as capable as their parents, while my daughter will need our help and guidance for many years to come. But this too makes evolutionary sense: one reason for our long infancy and childhood is to give the human mind time to adapt creatively to thousands of different circumstances. Pelicans, on the other hand, are ruled by a few simple laws and behaviors. Still, at the risk of romanticizing, I like the sense of calm the birds exude, the sense of timelessness, of ritual and grace.

We humans face a different set of problems. Our bodies still run on rhythms we only half understand (and often ignore), and we have adapted ourselves beyond ritual. To a certain extent all rules are off. The life of a hunter or farmer, the life that all humans lived until recently, directly connected us to the worlds of animals and plants, and to the cycles of the seasons. Without these primal guidelines, we are left facing a kind of uncertainty that on good days offers a multifarious delight of options, and on bad days offers chaos. Ungrounded in this new place, I am acutely sensitive to both possibilities. And while it isn't comfortable building a foundation on uncertainty, it has the advantage of being consistent with reality. Maybe in this world the best we can do is to not make false claims for certainty, and try to ride as gracefully as we can on the uncertain.

THE HUMAN brain is no match for depression, for the chaos of uprootedness. To try to turn our brains on ourselves, to think we can solve our own problems within ourselves, is to get lost in a hall of mirrors. But there is a world beyond the human world and that is a reason for hope. From a very selfish human perspective, we need more than the human.

Water and birds have always helped me live, have always lifted me beyond myself, and this morning I paddle out beyond the breakers and lie with my back to the surfboard just like the girl I saw in early fall. But while my legs may be crossed casually, I spend most of the time worrying about falling off. Even so, as I bob up and down on the waves, the whole ocean lifting and dropping below me, my niggling mind goes quiet for a minute. And then it goes beyond quiet. I'm thinking of Hadley, sitting up now and holding her own bottle, and I feel my chest fill with the joy these small achievements bring. She will be a strong girl I suspect, an athlete. And, no doubt, if we stay here she will become a surfer, delighting in her own *funktionslust*.

Glancing up at the pelicans flying overhead, I notice that there is something slightly backward-leaning about their posture, particularly when they are searching for fish, as if they were peering over spectacles. From directly below they look like giant kingfishers. But when they pull in their wings they change entirely: a prehistoric Bat Signal shining over Gotham. Then I see one bird with tattered feathers whose feet splay out crazily before he tucks to dive. When he tucks, dignity is regained, and the bird shoots into the water like a spear.

Inspired by that bird, I decide to turn my attention back to surfing. I catch a few waves, but catch them late, and so keep popping wheelies and being thrown off the surfboard. Then, after a while, I remember Matt telling me that I've been putting my weight too far back on the board. So on the next wave, almost without thinking, I shift my weight forward and pop right up. What surprises me most is how easy it is. I had allotted months for this advancement, but here I am, flying in toward the beach on top of a wave, its energy surging below. A wild giddiness fills me. It's cliché to say that I am completely in the present moment as this happens, and it's also not really true. Halfway to shore I'm already imagining telling Nina about my great success, and near the end of my ride, as the great wave deposits me in knee-deep water, I find myself singing the *Hawaii Five-O* theme song right out loud.

Though no one is around I let out a little hoot, and by the time I jump off the board I'm laughing out loud. A week ago I watched some kids, who couldn't have been older than twelve or thirteen, as they ran down the beach on a Friday afternoon. Happy that school was out, they sprinted into the water before diving onto their boards and gliding into the froth of surf. I'm not sprinting, but I do turn around and walk the surfboard back out until I am hip deep, momentarily happy to be the animal I am, my whole self buzzing from a ride that has been more the result of grace than effort. Then, still laughing a little, I climb on top of the board and paddle back into the waves.

I COULD end on that note of grace, but it wouldn't be entirely accurate. The year doesn't conclude triumphantly with me astride the board, trumpets blaring, as I ride that great wave to shore. Instead it moves forward in the quotidian way years do, extending deep into winter and then once again opening up into spring. As the days pass, my new place becomes less new, and the sight of the squadrons of pelicans loses some of its thrill. This too is perfectly natural, a process known in biology as habituation. Among both birds and humans, habituation is, according to my books, the "gradual reduction in the strength of a response due to repetitive stimulation." This is a fancy way of saying we get used to things.

While the pelican brain repeats ancient patterns, the human brain feeds on the new. On a biological level novelty is vital to the human experience: at birth the human brain is wired so that it is attracted to the unfamiliar. I see this in my daughter as she begins to conduct more sophisticated experiments in the physical world. True, all of these experiments end the same way, with her putting the object of experimentation into her mouth, but soon enough she will move on to more sophisticated interactions with her environment. She's already beginning to attempt language and locomotion. Although pelicans her age are already diving for fish, she, as a *Homo sapiens,* can afford to spot *Pelecanus occidentalis* a lead. She will gain ground later. Her long primate infancy will allow her relatively enormous brain to develop in ways that are as foreign to the birds as their simplicity is to us, and will allow that brain to fly to places the birds can never reach.

While I acknowledge these vast differences between bird and human, there is something fundamentally unifying in the two experiences of watching the pelicans and watching my daughter. There is a sense that both experiences help me fulfill Emerson's still-vital dictum: "First, be a good animal." For me fatherhood has intensified the possibility of loss, the sense that we live in a world of weak stability. But it has also given me a more direct connection to my animal self, and so, in the face of the world's chaos, I try to be a good animal. I get out on the water in an attempt to live closer to what the nature writer Henry Beston called "an elemental life."

I keep surfing into late fall, actually getting up a few times. But then one day I abruptly quit. On that day it is big, much too big for a beginner like me. I should understand this when I have trouble paddling out, the waves looming above me before throwing my board and self backward. And I should understand this as I wait to catch waves, the watery world lifting me higher than ever before. But despite the quiet voice that is telling me to go home I give it a try, and before I know it I am racing forward, triumphant and exhilarated, until the tip of my board dips under and the wave bullies into me from behind and I am thrown, rag-doll style, and held under by the wave. Then I'm tossed forward again and the board, tethered to my foot by a safety strap, recoils and slams into my head. I do not black out; I emerge and stagger to the shore, touching my hand to the blood and sand on my face. The next night I teach my Forms of Creative Nonfiction class with a black eye.

So that is enough, you see. One of the new territories I am entering is that of middle age, and the world doesn't need too many middle-aged surfers.

I feared fatherhood, but most of the results of procreation have been delightful ones. One exception, however, is the way that disaster seems to loom around every corner—disaster that might befall my daughter, my wife, myself. No sense adding "death by surfing" to the list.

WHILE I HAVE naturally begun to take the pelicans for granted, they still provide daily pleasures throughout the winter. What I lose in novelty, I gain in the early stages of intimacy. I see them everywhere: as I commute to work they fly low in front of my windshield; they placidly perch atop the pilings while I sip my evening beer on the dock near our house; they bank above me as I drive over the drawbridge to town. My research reveals that in March they begin their annual ritual of mating: a male offers the female a twig for nest-building and then, if she accepts, they bow to each other before embarking on the less elegant aspect of the ritual, the actual mating, which lasts no more than twenty seconds. These rituals are taking place, as they should, in privacy, twenty miles (thirty-two kilometers) south on a tiny island in the mouth of the Cape Fear River. The eggs are laid in late March or early April and a month-long period of incubation begins.

Around the midpoint of incubation, my human family achieves its own milestone. Throughout the spring I have continued to carry my daughter down the beach to watch the pelicans fish, but today is different from the other days. Today Hadley no longer rests in a pouch on my chest but walks beside me hand in hand. I remind myself that the mushiness I feel at this moment, the sensation that some describe as sentimentality, also serves an evolutionary purpose. With that softening comes a fierceness, a fierce need to protect and aid and sacrifice. This is not a theoretical thing but a biological one. In fact this transformation borders the savage, and here too the pelicans have long served humans as myth and symbol. "I am like a pelican of the wilderness," reads Psalm 102. At some point early Christians got it into their heads that pelicans fed their young with the blood from their own breasts, a mistake perhaps based on the red at the tip of some pelican bills, or, less plausibly, on their habit of regurgitating their fishy meals for their young. Whatever the roots of this misapprehension, the birds became a symbol of both parental sacrifice and, on a grander scale, of Christ's own sacrifice. The images of pelicans as self-stabbing birds, turning on their own chests with their bills, were carved in stone and wood and still adorn churches all over Europe. Later, the parental symbol was sometimes reversed, so that Lear, railing against his famous ingrate offspring, calls them "those pelican daughters."

THE YEAR culminates in a single day, a day full of green, each tree and bird defined sharply as if with silver edges. I kiss Nina and Hadley goodbye while they are still asleep and head out at dawn to the road where Walker will pick me up. Walker Golder is the deputy director of the North Carolina Audubon Society, a friend of a new friend, and today he takes me in a small outboard down to the islands at the mouth of the Cape Fear River. We bomb through a man-made canal called Snow's Cut and I smile stupidly at the clarity of the colors: the blue water, the brown eroding banks, the green above.

We stop at four islands. The southernmost of these is filled with ibis nests—11,504 to be exact. Ten percent of North America's ibises begin their lives here, and at one point we stand amid a snowy blizzard of birds, vivid white plumage and flaming bills swirling around us. Next we visit an island of terns, the whole colony seemingly in an irritable mood. This island, and its nearby twin, were formed when the river was dredged in the '70s by the U.S. Army Corps of Engineers, which used the sand to consciously aid the Audubon Society in an attempt to create nesting grounds. Terns, like ibises and pelicans, require isolated breeding areas, preferably islands, and this human experiment, this marriage of birders and engineers, has worked to perfection. We watch as a pair of royal terns spiral above us in their courtship dance.

The terns are impressive, but the highlight of the day for me is North Pelican Island, the nesting ground of almost all of the pelicans I have watched over the last year. Hundreds of pelicans sit on their ground nests, some of which are as big as beanbag chairs. They watch impassively as we approach. The old naturalists might have called these birds "undemonstrative" and "lugubrious," but I'll go with "calm." In fact, while we're anthropomorphizing, I might as well put "Buddha-like" in front of calm. It's hard not to project this on them after experiencing the wild defensiveness of the tern colony. The pelicans barely glance up at us. Theirs is a much different survival strategy, a much quieter one, but natural for such a big bird with no native predators on these islands. I crunch up through the marsh elder and phragmites to a spot where two hundred or so pelicans are packed together, sitting on their nests, incubating. Some still have the rich chestnut patches on the backs of their heads and necks, a delightful chocolate brown: leftover breeding plumage. They sit in what I now recognize as their characteristic manner, swordlike bills tucked into the fronts of their long necks.

While the birds remain quiet and calm, there is a sense of urgency here. This marsh island, like most of the islands that pelicans breed on, is very close to sea level. One moon-tide storm could wash over it and drown the season out. It is a time of year marked by both wild hope and wild precariousness, danger and growth going hand in hand. The birds are never more vulnerable, and as a father, I know the feeling.

I'm not sure exactly what I gain from intertwining my own life with the lives of the animals I live near, but I enjoy it on purely physical level. Maybe I hope that some of this calm, this sense of ritual, will be contagious. If the pelicans look lugubrious to some, their effect on me is anything but. And so I indulge myself for a moment and allow myself to feel unity with the ancient birds. It may sound trite to say that we are all brothers and sisters, all united, but it is also simply and biologically true. DNA undermines the myth of our species' uniqueness, and you don't need a science degree to reach this conclusion. We are animals, and when we pretend we are something better, we become something worse.

Having seen these fragile nesting grounds a thousand times before, Walker is to some extent habituated to them. He is also more responsible than any other human being for their protection. "We only visit briefly in the cool of the morning," he explains, "so not to disturb the birds." Playing tour guide, he walks in closer to the nests and gestures for me to follow. He points to some eggs that look anything but lusterless, and then to another nest where we see two birds, each just a day old. Though pelicans develop quickly, they are born featherless and blind, completely dependent on their parents, their lives a wild gamble. Heat regulation, Walker explains, is a big factor in nestling survival. Pelican parents must shade their young on hot days, and one dog let loose on this island while the owner gets out of his boat to take a leak could drive the parents from the nest, resulting in the deaths of hundreds of nestlings.

But we are not thinking about death, not right now. We are instead watching these tiny purple dinosaurs that could fit in the palm of your hand, the beginnings of their extravagant bills already in embryonic evidence. And then, in a neighboring nest an egg trembles. There's a tapping, and a pipping out from within.

A small blind purple head emerges from the shell. "Something only a mother could love," Walker says, and we laugh. But we are both in awe. It is the beginning of something, any idiot can see that. But what may be harder to see is that it is also a great and epic continuation.

While we watch, the almost-pelican cracks through the eggshell, furious for life. Then it shakes off the bits of shell and steps out into a new and unknown world.

WATCHING
BIRDS

A SOCIETY *of* MUTTONBIRDS

. . . .

(JOHN ALCOCK)

To reach Port Campbell National Park to the west of Melbourne, I must first navigate for an hour and a half across the city. Captain Cook felt no greater sense of relief upon securing his passage through the shoals of the Great Barrier Reef than I do upon weaving through the tumult of left-handed city traffic to reach the relative safety of the highways beyond.

The boats of Port Campbell rise and fall in the small and barely protected harbor, a notch in the huge yellow sea cliffs that run for miles along the coast here. Winds off a cold ocean have sheared the heathlands smooth. Here and there a stick of a tree twists and bends in a futile attempt to escape the force of the southerlies. Enormous breakers roll forward, pushed by the wind, to assault the massive barrier that confronts them. Waves erupt against rock, sending explosions of white sea spume into the air. Despite the apparent stability of the cliffs, the waves are winning, gradually consuming the land. Because the rock erodes unevenly, great stacks of stone remain scattered and abandoned in the blue-and-white ocean, surrounded by water, untoppled for the moment but marking the gradual victory of the sea.

Some of the vertical stacks have flat upper surfaces covered by an acre or so (half a hectare) of stunted heath, and these serve as nesting sites for the short-tailed shearwater. The shearwater gets its common name of "muttonbird" because the nestlings bulge with stored fat, and Australians have collected them for oil and food from colonial times to the present.

Muttonbird Island is cut off from the mainland by a narrow channel the waves have carved in recent geologic time. A side road from the coastal highway runs down to the ocean cliff near the stack and ends in a little car park on a tiny exposed promontory. From this point one can supposedly see the shearwaters. But the adult birds can be watched only in the evening when after a day spent at sea they return to dig their burrows in the ground or, later, to feed the single fat chick within their burrows.

Today, at the start of the breeding season, I wonder if the birds will appear on cue. A hard gale blows in from the southwest and the faint sun intermittently casts an unwholesome yellow-gray light on a steely ocean. A fine mist from waves broken on the cliff face swirls up two hundred feet (sixty meters), coating the windshield with a grimy salt film. The campervan rocks in the wind; on the radio a German poet discusses his epic work on the sinking of the *Titanic*.

A short instance from Muttonbird Island a deep and narrow trench digs into the cliffs. In the midst of a fierce winter storm in 1878, the *Loch Ard*, a magnificent clipper ship bound for Melbourne from London, ran aground on a reef about a half mile (nearly a kilometer) offshore. The ship's master had failed to see the Otway Light and had come too close to land. The *Loch Ard* quickly began to break apart, and the fifty-two people on board desperately launched lifeboats in the wind, fog, and blackness of the terrible sea. To see the surf erupting against the cliffs in daylight is proof that there could have been no hope for lifeboats headed toward that coast at night in even a moderate gale.

Two people miraculously survived, a sailor who was blown under an overturned lifeboat in the narrow inlet, now called Loch Ard Gorge, and a young woman clinging to a ship's spar who also slipped into the gorge. The woman did not reach the tiny sandy beach at the end of the cleft but was trapped against the cliff. The sailor heard her cries, and in the night he reentered the freezing water, overcame the battering waves, and rescued her.

On the radio the German poet explains that the *Titanic*'s fate is a metaphor for the destiny of modern society. I scan the ocean fruitlessly for shearwaters. Once a great white gannet cuts over the waves, riding the wind with swaggering ease on huge, black-tipped wings.

As dusk inches across the apparently lifeless ocean, a small black mote appears, so minute and so far away that it may only be a product of wishful thinking. But it is a shearwater. And soon a line of the birds materializes, then another, as if through spontaneous generation. The shearwaters cruise the ocean, tacking back and forth on sharp wings that almost touch the stormy surface of the sea as they carry the birds slowly toward the cliffs.

As evening arrives, shearwaters reach the stack and begin to rise far above the ocean in their approach to land. A few birds race with the wind and loop over the mainland before sailing back to Muttonbird Island. They strafe the island on black wings before fluttering down to disappear into the green heath. The wind continues its relentless attack. In the deepening evening, arriving shearwaters slide through the grayness, barely visible in the mist and the day's slow decay.

THE SHORT-TAILED shearwaters that swirled over Muttonbird Island on that stormy evening were the survivors of an extraordinary migration that is repeated every year by millions of adult birds. After the summer breeding season ends in April or May (autumn in the southern hemisphere), the shearwaters move to New Zealand's Tasman Sea and then go north across the equator to the northwestern corner of the Pacific Ocean. Later, in anticipation of a new breeding season, the birds permit westerlies to carry them across the Pacific and down along the west coast of North America. From there they swing back across the equatorial Pacific and over to eastern Australia, arriving at a multitude of muttonbird islands in September to renew the cycle.

The advantages to individuals of participating in such an extravagant migration, twenty thousand miles (30,000 kilometers) of traveling as a shearwater flies, must lie in the ability of migrant birds to feed both in southern and northern oceans at times when these waters are richest in marine life, while avoiding terrible winter storms. Shearwaters pay a large price to secure these benefits, for in some years vast numbers return to Australia so weakened by the long flight home that they perish without breeding, and their bodies wash up on Australian beaches amid the sea wrack.

At times on their migrations and during the breeding season, the birds are highly social, traveling in dense flocks of thousands, skimming over the waves, a few stiff wing-beats, then a long glide, a few more wingbeats, another long glide. Social life in fairy penguins appears to have evolved in response to the threat of predation. Could the same factor be responsible for the flocking behavior of short-tailed shear-waters? If the predation hypothesis is correct, there should be at least some observations of predators attacking shearwa-ters. The only predators that threaten migrating shearwaters might be the Pacific gull, white-breasted sea eagle, or per-egrine falcon. But these hunters operate close to shore, and if their actions over evolutionary time have favored shearwa-ters that clumped together to dilute the risk per individual of being killed in an attack, the tendency to flock should be greatest close to shore. The discovery of great flocks far out at sea would weaken the predation hypothesis (unless we also discovered special predators at work in pelagic environments).

But we must also consider alternative hypotheses for flocking that do not invoke predation. Perhaps individuals that group together can confuse and capture their prey more efficiently than isolated birds. Or perhaps one shearwater improves its flight efficiency by closely following another, if air that has passed over the lead bird's wings provides a more aerodynamic environment than unmodified turbulent air. (Long-distance migrants, such as Canada geese, that travel together in v formation can in theory fly 70 percent farther than a solo bird with the same energy expenditure because of drag reduction association with the v-flight pattern.)

Although the list of possible explanations for flocking in shearwaters could be expanded, we have looked at a sufficient number to demonstrate that hypotheses abound. What little evidence exists to help us discriminate among these ideas supports the predation hypothesis to some extent. The parallels with the unrelated fairy penguins are numerous. Like the penguins, shearwaters gather in the late afternoon near their burrows but do not approach shore until dusk has arrived. At times they can be seen floating on the water in great rafts, or simply drifting back and forth over the ocean, so the delay in landing has nothing to do with the necessity to hunt for food during every possible daylight hour. Instead it looks as if individuals wait until a great armada of shearwaters has assembled and until partial darkness impairs the vision of waiting gulls, hawks, and eagles before the shearwaters come ashore to the safety of their island burrows. Moreover, the *Complete Book of Australian Birds* claims that short-tailed shearwaters do not raft in places where predators are absent; if this could be carefully documented, it would provide extremely powerful support for the predation hypothesis as an explanation for flocking near the coast.

In light as dim as light can be, I strain to catch a last glimpse of a late-arriving muttonbird. The surf thunders against the coast. I am glad to be in the campervan and not on the *Titanic* or the *Loch Ard* just before they went down, when I would have had a chance to study the nature of social behavior in humans more closely than I desire.

OSPREY

· · · ·

(JENNIFER ACKERMAN)

THE TEMPERATURE this morning is 82 degrees Fahrenheit (28 degrees Celsius). The relative humidity is 85 percent. The wind is all by the sea; here in the bay it is quiet and warm. I've come to the cape in the hopes of seeing a pair of osprey, newly mated and nesting on a wooden platform by the bay. But the birds are nowhere in sight. Instead I spot a photographer in a three-piece suit, and his subjects, a groom in tails and a bride in a starchy white, high-necked gown. It is a pretty scene: Behind the pair, dunes stretch to the sea, patchy mats of beach heather exploding with the yellow bloom of May. But the bride seems annoyed. Her satin pumps fight the avalanching dunes, heels probing the sand like the bill of a willet. She reaches out to the groom to steady herself, removes a shoe, and empties a long stream of grit. She looks young, barely twenty. Beads of sweat soak the lace rimming her veil. The flies are up; the warm air carries the stench of creatures rotting on the flats.

Yesterday I was lucky enough to catch the ospreys copulating. Through my scope I could see the female in intimate detail perched on the edge of the platform, her glistening yellow eyes, the dusky shafts of her breastband, the soft green-gray of her feet. Her mate circled above, white belly shining in the sun. He whistled piercing notes, then dropped suddenly, dipping below the platform and swooping up to hover directly above her. He settled on her back gently, barely touching her with clenched talons, flapping his wings for balance. She tipped forward slightly, raising her tail high to the side to receive him. I watched, a little ashamed of my magnified view. They coupled in silence for twenty or thirty seconds. Then the female, with a light flutter of wings, shrugged off her mate, who slowly banked upward and slipped sidewise across the sky.

The osprey leapt into my heart from my first days here. For one thing, the big bird is easy to identify. So many shorebirds are what ornithologists call "LBJs," little brown jobs. These I tried to pin down in my notes with some vague hope of identifying them later. But the osprey's size, its white belly and dark carpal patches, its wings kinked at the wrist, gave it away. So did its slow whistled call, a penetrating *kyew, kyew,* which drifts down from overhead. I occasionally mistook a high-flying osprey for a gull, but eventually learned to read its pattern of flight: shallow wingbeats interspersed with long glides. Its movement was more purposeful and deliberate than a gull's, less flighty. The osprey's huge nests, most of them in open, public places, and its showy method of hunting—a dazzling power dive ending in a burst of spray—made it a conspicuous neighbor, familiar and expected.

WHEN I was seven or eight I went bird-watching with my father from time to time. I remember rising before dawn reluctantly and heading out, stiff, sleepy, my shoes damp with dew. In a family of five girls, time alone with my dad was a rare pleasure, not to be missed. The two of us would feel our way along the towpath between the C & O Canal and the Potomac River, cool breeze on the backs of our necks, companionable in late starlight. We moved quietly, all eyes for the small woodland birds we hoped to spy from a distance. It would begin with one bird, maybe two, chipping away at the dark. Then the clear whistled note of a cardinal would rise and the trilling of a wood thrush, and the songs would pass from one bird to another, their swelling sounds lifting me up by my ears. As the stars faded and branches emerged against the sky, sudden small shapes would appear and disappear, fluttering and darting about, flashing between the leaves: sparrows, finches, warblers, which I could just barely make out in the darkness. I didn't try to identify them. At that hour the world was theirs. On the ride home in the car, I would sift through my father's well-thumbed volume of Roger Tory Peterson's *Field Guide to North American Birds*, neatly indexed with plastic tabs marking the division of families: *Paridae* (titmice), *Sittidae* (nuthatches), *Troglodytidae* (wrens), and *Parulidae* (wood warblers). I was a pushover for the neat little manual, a fine tool for thinking about diversity and order in the world.

What birds I saw on those excursions were mostly wood-land species. When it came to shorebirds I was utterly lost. Some species were easy to pin down. The ruddy turnstone, for instance—a squat, aggressive little bird with a harlequin mask—or the black-bellied plover, with its long, elegant black bib. But the sandpipers were a different story. Peterson calls the littlest ones "peeps," the white-rumped, the semi-palmated, the least. There are rules, of course—the least is the smallest, its diminutive size earning it the species name *minutilla;* the semipalmated has a shorter, stouter bill—but judging either bill or body size at a distance seemed hopeless. Then there was the matter of plumage, which changes from season to season like foliage and which differs from male to female, from juvenile to immature to adult. Same bird, different disguises. No sooner had I nailed down the vari-ous appearances of one migratory species than another had taken its place. It's no wonder Aristotle came up with the theory of transmutation: Birds change species with the sea-sons, he said. Redstarts, common in Greece throughout the summer, became robins in winter; summer garden warblers changed into winter black caps. He claimed to have seen the birds midway in their metamorphoses. Anyone who has tried to identify fall birds in their shabby molting plumage can understand the mistake.

I eventually found a tutor in Bill Frech, a kind, owlish man, now eighty, who has been a devoted observer of winged things since he was twelve. Bill is up and away every morning at dawn to make his rounds in a vw with a scope mounted on the window. Though he claims not to have any special knowledge of winds or weather, he knows where the birds will be on any particular day, where heavy rains form pools of standing water that draw glossy ibises and egrets, which hay fields have been cut over recently, making good habitat for golden plovers, which buoys offer refuge to storm petrels in heavy wind. He sees what he sees, he says, and a good part of his pleasure is in the chanciness of the enterprise. One morning might yield nothing more interesting than a common goldeneye or an upland plover, while the next turns up a stray swallow-tailed kite hovering over the Lewes water tower, an Australian silver gull, or two thousand gannets riding out a storm behind Hen and Chickens Shoal.

Bill sees the world of light and motion not in a continuum, he says, but in frozen frames, a series of discernible stopwatch tableaux, which helps him spot his quarry. He scours the edges of the land, the broad sweep of sky and sea, one section at a time, and nearly always turns up a bird. I have tried to learn to do this, to look for spots of stillness on the tossing sea, for movement among the stubble of a cut field, but I often miss the mark and must have my eye directed. Bill carries no field guides. He depends less on fieldmarks to identify a bird than on its jizz, a term that comes from the fighter pilot's acronym GIS for General Impression and Shape. He has taught me to recognize a semipalmated plover or to distinguish a yellowlegs from a willet without quite knowing how I do so, just as one recognizes a friend from a distance not by individual characteristics, but by shape and gait. Most sandpipers walk and probe, while the plover runs and pecks; runs and pecks. Spotted sandpipers teeter. The Maliseet Indians of Maine understood this. They called the bird *nan a-mik-tcus,* or "rocks its rump." The sanderling flies steadily along; the plover's flight is wilder, full of tilting twists and turns.

Most warblers dart through trees, but myrtle warblers drift. Knowing the jizz of a bird is especially useful when it comes to identifying high-flying species: Canada geese flap constantly; cormorants glide, long black necks in eternal pursuit of tiny tufted heads; gannets dip like goldfinches; pelicans alternate flaps with a short sail. As Bill filled my head with these rules of thumb, the species slowly separated and gained names.

I HAVE the good fortune to live within a three-mile (five-kilometer) radius of five active osprey nests. One sits atop a platform on the double cross-arms of an old utility pole in the marsh at the center of town, hard by a railroad and King's Highway. The highway carries the crush of traffic disgorged from the Cape May–Lewes ferry, a steady stream of tourists hell-bent for a seaward peep. Another nest occupies a channel marker, a fancy site complete with a flashing red light powered by a solar panel and two bright orange warning signs. The rest sit on duckblinds and man-made platforms. The ospreys seem unbothered by all the human activity surrounding these sites. They are adaptable, versatile sorts, with a predilection for human ruins. An unkempt chimney, a vacant house, or a pile of fence rails gone back to nature draws them in. On an island in the Chesapeake Bay that was once a bombing range, ospreys nest on the busted-up car bodies used as targets. One pair set up housekeeping on the surface of an unexploded thousand-pound (450-kilogram) bomb.

Every year, within a day or two of St. Patrick's Day, as schooling fish move into the sun-warmed waters of the bay, the ospreys arrive on the south wind for the breeding season.

They fly in high and circle overhead, greeting each mudbank, each twist of creek with a high, clear whistle. Invariably a notice appears in the local paper: "The fishhawk, Delaware's harbinger of spring, has finally arrived."

The spectacle of courtship follows soon after. The young male selects a nesting site and then begins an aerial display, a slow, undulating flight high in the sky. Once an understanding is struck between a male of good property and his discriminating partner, nest building begins. The pair is up and down, in and out all day, scouring the neighborhood for appropriate materials. Ospreys are pack rats and indefatigable renovators. Though they nest in the same site from year to year, the nests themselves are often destroyed between seasons and so need considerable repairs. The birds don't seem particularly interested in permanence or stability. John Muir purportedly rode out a hurricane sitting on an eagle's nest. Ornithologist Alan Poole said he wouldn't trust his weight to an osprey nest on a blue windless day. At the nest near King's Highway, I've watched males bring in cornstalks, cow dung, crab shells, a fertilizer bag, a toy shovel, a slice of floor mat, and the doilylike remnants of fish net. Even this eclectic nest doesn't hold a candle to one John Steinbeck found in his Long Island garden, which contained three shirts, a bath towel, an arrow, and a rake.

The male plays hod carrier to the female's bricklayer. She has definite ideas about how things should be arranged and fulfills her task with zeal. The loose mass grows up and out until it looms like a giant mushroom cap against the horizon. Nest finished, the female turns broody, sitting deep in the nest cup so that only her head shows. The male brings her fish and often spells her while she perches nearby and consumes her meal head first, with a kind of horrible delicacy.

When I'm at a loss to explain some bit of bird biology or behavior I've observed, I turn to Arthur Cleveland Bent's mighty twenty-volume series on the *Life Histories of North American Birds*. (Bill Frech started acquiring copies of the books in the 1920s, when the U.S. Government Printing Office sent them out free. He got all but the last three volumes, which he had to buy from the publisher.) The organization of these volumes is tidy and pleasing. The section on ospreys, for instance, lists the bird's full Latin name, *Pandion haliaëtus carolinensis*. Then the common name, from the Latin *ossifraga,* or sea eagle. Then come sections filled with copious details on courtship, nesting, plumage, voice, enemies, and eggs, all enhanced by the observations of a large company of tipsters. Here's Mr. Clinton C. Abbott's catalogue of osprey calls:

> The commonest note is a shrill whistle, with a rising inflection: *Whew, whew, whew, whew, whew, whew, whew.* This is the sound usually heard during migration; and when the bird is only slightly aroused. When she becomes thoroughly alarmed it will be: *Chick, chick, chick, cheek, cheek, ch-cheek, ch-cheek, cheereek, chezeek, chazeek,* gradually increasing to a frenzy of excitement at the last. Another cry sounds like: *Tseep, tseep, tseep-whick, whick, whick-ick-ick-ck-ck,* dying away in a mere hiccough.

It is no easy task to record bird sound on paper, and you have to admire the efforts of Abbott. One crochety contributor expresses disappointment in this range: "All these notes . . . seem inadequate to express the emotions of so large a bird."

For the latest field studies on ospreys, I turn to Alan Poole's book, *Ospreys: A Natural and Unnatural History.* Here are hundreds of businesslike facts: the number of minutes of hunting necessary to meet the daily food requirements of an osprey family (195), the percentage of eggs lost from an average clutch in New York (68) and in Corsica (21), the total population of breeding pairs in Britain (45) and along the Chesapeake Bay (1,500).

According to both Bent and Poole, ospreys are traditional, one could even say conservative, birds. A female selects her mate not by his fancy flight, melodious song, or flamboyant feathers, but by his choice of homes. The birds favor the top limbs of large, mature, isolated trees. In a typical old-growth forest, fewer than one in a thousand trees suit. On this coast, where mature forests are mostly gone, the birds resort to distinctly unnatural sites: telephone poles, channel markers, fishing piers, and duck blinds. They favor overwater sites, which offer good protection from raccoons and other four-footed predators, but are of no use against winged carnivores such as the great horned owl. I've seen these formidable hunters perched on the Lewes water tower, heard them caterwauling in the dark, and found their pellets in the pine forest, packed solid with bones, feathers, and fur.

Ospreys are thought to mate for life. However, a recent story in *The New York Times* tells me that there is almost no such thing as true monogamy in the animal kingdom. It reports that scientists are uncovering evidence of philandering in species after species, withering the notion of lovingly coupled birds. With sophisticated spying techniques, they are spotting members of supposedly faithful pairs—purple martins, barn swallows, black-capped chickadees—flitting off for extramarital affairs. With DNA fingerprinting, they've compiled dossiers on the adulterers. One of the few known examples of true monogamy, they say, is a rodent living in the weeds and grasses of the midwestern prairies, a homely little vole called *Microtus ochrogaster,* which is utterly committed to its mate.

Still, it is fairly well established that adultery is rare among ospreys, and there are stories of fervent conjugal devotion. Bent reports the story of a bird whose mate was killed when a bolt of lightning struck her nest. The male refused to abandon the site, perching in a nearby tree all summer, a bird-shaped picture of bereavement. He returned the following year and stood vigil for another season.

A typical osprey clutch consists of three eggs, which Bent describes as "the handsomest of all the hawks' eggs . . . roughly the size of a hen's egg." Bent collected eggs most of his life, saved the orbs as trophies, laying their speckles in a cabinet fragrant with that peculiar pungent egg odor. "I shall never forget my envious enthusiasm," he writes, "when a rival boy collector showed me the first fish hawk's eggs I had ever seen." He goes on to describe the range of their appearance in loving detail: "The shell is fairly smooth and finely granulated. The ground color . . . may be white, creamy white, pinkish white, pale pinkish cinnamon, fawn color, light pinkish cinnamon, or vinaceous-cinnamon. They are usually heavily blotched and spotted with dark rich browns or bright reddish browns, bone brown, liver brown, bay, chestnut, burnt sienna, or various shades of brownish drab."

It was after reading this description that I bought a scope to watch more closely the activities of the ospreys nesting near King's Highway. I couldn't see the eggs themselves: They sat too low in the nest. But sometime late in the second week of June, they hatched. The newborn chicks were unfinished things, fuzzy flesh poking up from the bottom of the nest, as naked and helpless as a human baby, and no less perishably tender. Unlike such precocial birds as plovers and sandpipers, which go forth into the world straight from the egg, young ospreys take some coddling. Despite a steady stream of fish delivered by its parents, one chick died ten days later. The survivor, a fat squab with golden pinfeathers and thick black eye stripes, turned mobile at about four weeks, pestering its mother for fish and backing up now and again to squirt feces over the nest's edge. By midsummer, fatted on shad and flounder, puffed up on menhaden, it was flapping its scrawny wings, testing flight.

One warm, still day later that summer, I watched a young osprey fishing in the bay. The water was alive with hundreds of small silver fish that split the calm, sun-smooth surface. The bird flew in high from the southwest, slowly spiraled down to seventy or eighty feet (twenty to twenty-five meters), and began to stalk the shallows. The bright eye opened, the head lowered, the wings folded, then the feet thrust forward and the bird dropped like a feathered bomb, striking the water with a burst of spray.

Millions of generations of natural selection have made these birds good at what they do. Though ospreys have been known to take snakes, turtles, voles, and even baby alligators, 99 percent of their diet is fish, and they play every piscine angle. They spot fish from hundreds of feet above the water, even bottom fish with superb camouflage, like flounder. They penetrate the sun's glare or a dark, rippled water surface and adjust their strike to compensate for light refraction. With an eye membrane called a pecten, they change focus instantly to keep the fish in perfect view as they plunge. They hit the water at speeds of twenty to forty miles per hour (thirty to sixty kilometers per hour). Their dense, compact plumage protects against the force of the impact; a flap of tissue on top of the beak closes over the nostrils to shut out the splash. The bird's strong, sinewy legs are superbly adapted for catching and holding slippery prey. Sharp talons, curved and of equal length, can snap shut in a fiftieth of a second. One toe swings back so that the osprey can clutch its prey with two claws on either side. Short spines on the base of the bird's toes and footpads ensure a firm grip.

With several deep wingbeats, this young bird rose slowly, shook its wings, and shifted the wildly flapping quiver of silver in its broad talons so that it rode headfirst, like a rudder. I watched until nothing could be seen of it but the dark v-sign of wings against the sky.

ALDO LEOPOLD once wrote about the physics of beauty in the sand hills of Wisconsin. "Everybody knows... that the autumn landscape in the north woods is the land, plus a red maple, plus a ruffed grouse. In terms of conventional physics, the grouse represents only a millionth of either the mass or the energy of an acre. Yet subtract the grouse and the whole thing is dead... A philosopher has called this imponderable essence the *numenon* of material things." For me, the osprey supplies the same kind of motive power to this place.

In the 1950s and '60s, this coast nearly lost its numenon to DDT, what Rachel Carson called the "elixir of death." March brought few homecomers, June grew no aerie. The toxic brew did more damage to the osprey than had been done by decades of egg collecting, hunting, and habitat destruction.

During World War II, the U.S. Army had used DDT to combat body lice among its troops, successfully breaking the chain of typhus infection. After the war, farmers and government workers began using the pesticide as a weapon against mosquitoes and agricultural pests. Its hazards were recognized from the beginning. Two researchers from the U.S. Fish and Wildlife Service published a paper in 1946 warning of the dangers of DDT. They had found that spraying in New Jersey endangered blue crabs. In Pennsylvania, it was brook trout; in Maryland, birds, frogs, toads, snakes, and fish. Still, for almost three decades, most of the East Coast's shoreline and marshes were blanketed with DDT in an effort to eradicate the common salt-marsh mosquito. Long-lasting and easily dispersed, the pesticide spread over the earth in much the same pattern as radioactive fallout, carried aloft by wind and deposited on the ground in rainfall. By the 1960s, it permeated wildlife all around the globe, even lodging in tissues of Adelie penguins in Antarctica.

The highest concentrations of DDT residues were found in carnivorous birds at the top of the food chain: bald eagles, peregrine falcons, ospreys. The pesticide found its way into plankton and phytoplankton (microscopic plants and algae such as diatoms and dinoflagellates), which were eaten by shellfish, insects, and other creatures, which were eaten by fingerlings, which were in turn eaten by larger fish, which were caught by osprey. The concentration of the pesticide increased as much as ten times with each level in the chain. (Fish also accumulate toxins by absorbing pollutants directly through their gills.) What started out as a minute amount of DDT in water or plants ended up as a big dose in fish and an even bigger dose in the fatty tissues of birds of prey.

Ospreys can rid themselves of small amounts of some toxins: mercury, for instance. They excrete it from the blood into growing feathers, which are eventually molted—a technique that works only during the molting season. But mercury occurs in nature; DDT is man-made. Birds have had no time to evolve a way to rid their bodies of the poison. As the toxin accumulates in fatty tissues, it blocks the efficient metabolism of calcium and so makes the shell of an osprey's egg brittle, cracked by a touch of fingers. When a female settles down to incubate, she crushes her clutch beneath her.

Around the turn of the century, the ornithologist Alexander Wilson remarked that he saw osprey "thick about Rehoboth Bay," some twenty nests within a half-mile (one kilometer) range. A concentrated colony flourished then at Cape Henlopen, with twenty-three nesting pairs, probably drawn by the dense schools of menhaden that crowded the waters of the lower bay. By 1972, when DDT was finally banned in the United States, populations of ospreys here and elsewhere along the northeast coast had plummeted to a small fraction of their former numbers. When Bill Frech came to Lewes in 1977, there were forty-six nesting pairs of osprey in all of Delaware. That year, observers across the bay at Cape May counted just over a thousand migrating osprey during the whole autumn season. Since the 1970s, the birds have somehow recovered their numbers. In October of 1989, nearly a thousand birds were spotted passing through Cape May on a single day. At last count, Delaware had seventy-five nests.

MOST OSPREYS along this coast make impressive annual migrations in orbit with the seasons, traveling south to the tropics in fall and north again in spring to breed. Young birds travel both ways alone. The migration route they follow is not learned, but acquired in the egg, carried in them by the accident of ancestry. A young osprey fledged in Lewes goes south to Peru or Venezuela to winter in the hot mists and vast swamps of the Amazon, and returns after a year or two to breed on the very same stretch of temperate shore where it fledged.

I know the gift of being able to find home is not allotted merely to these birds. Moose return annually to the same summer range. Bears transported more than fifty miles (eighty kilometers) from their territory come back to it within days. Something in the cold brains of sea turtles guides them to their natal beaches after prodigious migrations of thousands of miles. Even limpets seem to know their way home, crawling back to a favorite scar or dimple on a rock at low tide, even if the face of the rock they cross has been hammered or chiseled into oblivion. Terns, swallows, gulls, and song sparrows, as well as shorebirds—piping plovers, ruddy turnstones, and sanderlings—all return to the same nesting ground in what is called *ortstreue,* or "place faithfulness." A strong attachment to birthplace makes good biological sense, of course. In a familiar landscape, animals have an easier time finding nesting sites and prey and avoiding predators. Biologist Ernst Mayr once remarked that birds have wings not so much for the purpose of getting away to a place but for the purpose of getting home.

Still, it seems astonishing that a young osprey, only a few months old, can take off over land and water and travel south three thousand miles (five thousand kilometers); then, years later, head sure and direct, without guidance, back to the precise point of its infancy. Scientists believe that members of a pair stay together because they share a deep affinity for the same stretch of marsh or shore. Apparently ospreys carry an image of home in their heads that is sharp and well defined. How does a young bird register this place? What are its landmarks of sight and smell? Is it, as Lamarck said, that the environment creates the organ? Does our particular wash of blue and white bore those bright golden eyes and code the neurons that stream into those kinked wings? Do our mottled currents and patterns of marsh grass brand a bird, saying, Come toward this shore? There may be other sensual messages sent by the earth, undetected by us, but which a bird is innately prepared to receive. Although scientists suspect that some consciousness of the exact magnetic topology and field strength of a nesting area has something to do with it, no one really knows. "It's a black box sort of thing," one ornithologist told me. Somehow this stretch of shore works a kind of magic against all others to pull its progeny from the sky.

WHEN I was twelve, the school I went to sat on a hillside near a mature deciduous wood. At lunchtime, I often retreated to a small clearing some distance from the school to eat my sandwich and reflect on the morning's events. One day I sat on a log, peeling bark from a stick, and pondering the news that had struck our family a few weeks before: my father was leaving my mother. It was a warm, breezy day. Sunlight moving in and out of the clouds shattered the leafy surfaces with flecks of gold. I hadn't noticed trouble between my parents, engrossed as I was in my own awkward passing into adolescence. No shouting, no slamming doors. Suddenly this. The sunglasses my mother had been wearing for days couldn't conceal from me her wet face, her bafflement and sense of betrayal. I was at that age when I yearned above all else to be invisible, the way a Fowler's toad is invisible against the sand of the pine forest floor. The rift between my parents made me stand out and pick sides. It set me adrift, hunting for stable sanctuary in what had come to seem a shifting, unreliable world.

These woods were comforting and familiar. I knew their mossy hummocks and decaying stumps as well as any place I'd ever known. But this day I saw something new. Glancing up from the stick in my hand, I noticed a vibrating white dot about the size of a firefly in the trunk of an oak tree some distance from where I sat. It was more an absence than a presence, a tiny pulsating hole. I stared and stared. The hole slowly grew into a crescent, then a large ragged horseshoe, a sizeable bite that should have split the tree in two. But the top half of the trunk just hung there like a stalactite. Still the hole grew, spreading in pulses until it swallowed nearby bushes and trees in white-hot light. It was as if my woods were being punched out or sucked up in a shiny boiling void. I couldn't shift my gaze from the growing hole, and a sense of horror stole over me. I got up and stumbled blindly out of the woods. By this time my hands were numb, dead weight at the ends of my arms, like dangling lumps of dough. Nausea roiled my insides; then a dot of hot pain shot through my temple and set the right side of my head throbbing.

This was my first experience with the aura of a classical migraine headache. The visual disturbance, the scintillating, zigzaggy chasm, is called a scotoma, meaning darkness or shadow. I rarely have such attacks anymore. I've learned to fend them off by lying down in darkness and focusing on that first tiny flash of white light, concentrating it until it shrinks into a pinpoint and pops out of existence. But I still think of that first aura not merely as a chaotic burst of firing among the thin wires of my brain but as a sudden, complete extinction of place.

Oddly enough, that pleat in my perception held a vision of the future. Several years later, when I returned to visit those woods, I found them gone. In their place was a thick cluster of row houses that clung like barnacles to the edge of the hill, and I was struck anew by a sense of disorientation and loss.

This sensation is not peculiar to humans. The loss of familiar surroundings, the destruction of refuge, is no doubt felt by animals, perhaps even more keenly than by our kind. I once saw something like this happen to a pair of osprey that for more than a decade had nested on a dilapidated pier behind the old fish factories. The pier was used in the 1950s and '60s to offload the giant nets of menhaden. When the factories closed, the pier fell into disuse; all that was left was a set of rotting pilings with a few cross timbers, disconnected from the land. One fall, developers bulldozed the fish factories to build condominiums and tore up the old pier. When the osprey returned that March, I watched them circle the empty water for hours in bewilderment. They hung around for days, perching on a nearby utility pole and watching the site, apparently recollecting a structure now made of air.

Stories are told of species that retain an image in their heads of places that have long disappeared. Monarchs migrating over Lake Superior fly south, then east, then south again, as if reading the echoes of a long-vanished glacier. Year after year, pilot whales on their autumn migrations strand themselves on the beaches of Cape Cod, as if unwilling to accept the presence of a twelve-thousand-year-old geological upstart that has parked itself in the middle of a migratory path they have followed for millions of years. American toads return to breed in ponds that have long since been paved over, drawn by some insubstantial vapor, some aura of home.

STUDIES OF human preferences for landscapes have found that our tribe tends to favor savannalike land—flat, grass-covered landscape studded with trees, where we had our origins and earliest home. Also promontories overlooking water. Some scientists even speculate that somewhere along the way we veered off the common primate course of evolution not just by swinging down from trees, but by going toward the sea. The seashore, with its abundance of edibles— fish, mollusks, turtle and bird eggs, digestible plants—and of shells, vines, kelp, and driftwood for tools, was the home of emergent humanity.

I like this idea that our earliest home landscapes are buried deep, embedded in our minds like an anchor at great depth, that we know in some dark, birdly way where we want to go.

Beauty may, indeed, lie in the genes of the beholder. Ospreys have been around for something like fifteen million years, long before we ever set foot on seashores. In our burgeoning minds, shore has never been separate from bird, so perhaps at some level, the two are joined in an inexplicable sweetness of union. Perhaps the osprey exists on a mental map of an earlier world passed down from our ancestors, and the bird in its landscape enters us like the parental. Perhaps it is also the other way around: Perhaps *he* contains *us* as part of his element, having seen us through the ages, through our infancy and the whole tumult of civilized man.

I wonder, too, if the residues of old ancestral landscapes don't rise up in our minds by the same deep grooves that make the scent of hay or sunlit ferns call up an episode from childhood, so that we act on buried instinct—like a dog at the hearth who turns slowly around and around on himself, tamping down a circle of imaginary grass—so that for the sake of marking her union in a meaningful way, a young bride puts up with salt stench and sand in her shoe.

THE COLOR *of a* BIRD'S EGG

. . . .

(BERND HEINRICH)

THE FOUR tiny eggs that were cradled on feathers in a nest of moss, lichens, and spiderwebs were more beautiful than anything I had ever seen. They were greenish blue, marked with purple and lavender blotches and black scratchy squiggles. The cascading songs of a chaffinch rang exuberantly from the forest on that beautiful spring morning, and I knew I had discovered paradise.

I was eight years old, and with Papa's bedtime stories of his adventures collecting the eggs of rare waterbirds in the swamps of the Danube delta inflaming my mind, I was hooked. I became obsessed with finding the nests and eggs of more and more species. Each one was a triumph, and a lesson in ornithology, because each species has its own intricate and individual behavior that must be learned before you can find its nest.

I still treasure these jewels, but now I do not arrange them in glass-covered boxes. Instead, I photograph and file their essence in my mind, and sometimes in scientific journals. The filing system I use is based on evolution, and it reveals levels of reality and beauty that were never imagined by Papa, or me. I now see the beauty of the eggs not only in nests in the field but also in the analyses of dedicated researchers.

First, you see the diversity. The eggs of the scarlet tanager, in a cup of loose twigs lined with dark rootlets, are sky blue and spotted with light brown in a ring at the larger end. Crows' and ravens' eggs are olive green with gray and black splotches and dots. The eggs of the eastern peewee are a light cream, with a wreath of reddish-brown and lavender spots about the larger end. These colors are set against a round nest-cup decorated with gray-green lichens. Woodpecker and kingfisher eggs—from holes excavated in trees and sandbanks, respectively—are translucent white and without any trace of markings. The different colors, or lack of them, are all products of evolution. How did they come to be? What were the selective pressures that generated them?

The combinations of markings and colors on birds' eggs may seem like creativity gone berserk. Why should the color of an eggshell matter? Why, indeed, have any color at all? There must have been reasons to add the color, or else specialized glands to apply color would not have evolved after the reptile ancestors of birds no longer buried or covered their eggs. So why are catbirds' eggs a bright, almost luminescent, blue, flickers' eggs pure white, and the loons' eggs a dark olive green?

Birds' eggs are marked by pigments secreted from the walls of the oviduct. They are uncolored before being laid and become painted when traversing the uterus; the pressure of the egg squeezes pigment out of the uterine glands onto the eggshell, and the motion of the egg affects the color patterns. It is as if innumerable brushes hold still while the canvas moves. If the egg remains still, there are spots, and if it moves while the glands continue secreting, then lines, scrawls, and squiggles result.

There is considerable genetic plasticity in egg color. Some strains of domestic chickens have the familiar white and brown eggs. Others have been bred that lay eggs tinted blue, green, or olive.

It is not surprising that Charles Darwin, with his wide-ranging interests, also thought about the adaptive significance of the coloration of birds' eggs. Since coloration is generally absent in the eggs of hole nesters— for example, woodpeckers, parrots, kingfishers, barbets, and honeyguides—he supposed that the pigmentation on the eggs of open nesters acts as a sunscreen to protect the embryo. The British ornithologist David Lack, in turn, believed the white coloration of eggs of most hole nesters allowed the birds to see their eggs in the dark. Yet even if it is advantageous for birds to see their eggs in the dark (which I doubt), we still have to explain the tremendous differences in colors and patterns, especially in the species that do *not* nest in holes. Why isn't one sunscreen best? And if one is, why don't all use it? And why are some hole nesters' eggs spotted? Perhaps, as Austin L. Rand, the former chief curator of zoology at the Field Museum in Chicago, has said, "Like some of the specific differences in nest building, variations in egg color are simply expressions of the general tendency of birds toward diversity." This idea, too, might be right, but if so it is only a small part of the elephant that the proverbial blind men try to describe by touch.

Nobody who has seen the drab buff, black-blotched eggs of a killdeer on a sandbar or the olive-green eggs of a snipe in a sedge meadow, or who has walked the tundra and flushed the semipalmated sandpiper and golden plover out of their nest, will doubt that one function of egg color is camouflage.

Experiments confirm that the color of some birds' eggs conceals them from predators. In one famous experiment, the Dutch Nobel laureate and ethologist Niko Tinbergen distributed equal numbers of naturally spotted eggs of black-headed gulls, uniformly khaki-colored eggs, and white eggs near a gull colony and then recorded the predation by carrion crows and herring gulls on these unguarded eggs. The spotted eggs suffered the least predation.

We might reasonably assume that the darkly blotched and spotted markings of snipe, killdeer, and gull eggs function as camouflage, and that they evolved under selective pressure from visually oriented egg predators. But why then do other ground-nesting birds, such as most ducks and many grouse, have *unmarked* eggs—eggs that cannot be considered camouflaged by any stretch of the imagination? Perhaps part of the answer is that most of these birds hide their nests in dense vegetation, and the incubating female's own body is camouflaged, and she sits on them or buries them with nest lining.

A pet mallard hen gave me the suggestion that this was so. The downy mallard chicks had been an Easter present for my daughter Erica, and they soon grew into ducks. The hen built a nest by scraping leaves together under a bush by the front window. Being well fed, she laid enormous clutches of creamy pale-green eggs. But I never saw the eggs uncovered. Each morning before she left, after laying an egg, she used her bill to pull leaves from around the nest to cover the eggs completely. The leaves were better camouflage than spots on the eggs could ever be. Years later, when my nephew Charlie and I made a canoe trip down the Naotak River, in Alaska, I found several willow ptarmigan nests, their numerous eggs heavily blotched and marbled with blackish-brown markings. I predicted that such camouflage indicated that the eggs would not be covered up during the week or more it takes to accumulate a full clutch, before incubation can begin. What a thrill it was to find that this was so! The nests were always in scrapes of pebbles and debris, where there was no material (such as leaves or grass) to cover them.

Many birds with nests that have no loose material with which to cover the eggs also have unmarked, uncamouflaged eggs. They include hummingbirds, pigeons, and doves. But these birds lay only two eggs per clutch, and they incubate as soon as the *first* egg is laid. Perhaps because none of their eggs is normally left uncovered for long, there has been no need to color them for camouflage.

This is probably the best explanation for the lack of color and markings on hole nesters' eggs and those of birds that lay small clutches: there was no need for color, so none evolved. Yet some birds—such as chickadees, nuthatches, and wrens—nest in holes yet still lay spotted eggs. (True hole nesters excavate their own holes and lay white eggs without adding any nest material.) I suspect, therefore, that the spots on the eggs of these birds are evolutionary baggage. They tell us that these species were previously open nesters who switched to hole nesting, or to building nests with a roof, in more recent evolutionary time. They retained the habit of building nests, as well as the coloration of their eggs, because there was no great selective pressure for change.

While the coloring and markings of birds' eggs function primarily as camouflage, they can also have the opposite function. On our Atlantic and Pacific coasts, on adjacent islands, and in Europe, murres nest on ledges and sea cliffs in colonies of hundreds of thousands. Several species of colonial cliff-nesting murres (as was also true of the extinct great auk) have eggs that vary widely in color and markings. The ground color of the eggs may be creamy, white, reddish, warm ocher, pale blue, or even deep greenish blue. The markings upon this ground color may be blotches, spots, or intricate interlacing lines of yellowish brown, bright red, dark brown, or black. Some eggs are unmarked. When a murre loses its one egg—its entire clutch—it lays another, and this one is colored like the first. In contrast, the closely related auklets of various species nest in burrows or rock crevices; the nest entrance serves to identify a bird's clutch of eggs, and so the individual eggs need no markings to be identified in the vast assemblage of others.

Chester A. Reed, an oologist during the heyday of egg collecting, in the last century, says of the murres: "The eggs are laid as closely as possible on the ledges where the incubating birds sit upright, in long rows like an army on guard. As long as each bird succeeds in finding an egg to cover on its return home, it is doubtful if the bird either knows, or cares, whether it is its own or not." Thanks to experiments by the biologist Beat Tschantz, of the Zoological Institute of the University of Bern, we know that Reed was wrong. Murres no more incubate one another's eggs than lobstermen tend one another's traps. Both use color markings to identify their property. Tschantz switched eggs and found that if an egg of a different color or marking pattern was substituted for the bird's own egg, that egg was rejected, but another egg with a similar pattern was accepted. However, the birds don't know *a priori* what color egg they produce. Egg color is learned. For example, if a murre's first egg is marked with white feces in small increments, the bird learns that color pattern and will reject eggs of its own pattern. This acute ability of murres to differentiate eggs by their color stands in strong contrast to the behavior of some birds—herring gulls, for example—which accept almost anything even remotely resembling an egg, of any color.

Reproductive success in murres is enhanced if the females can pick our their own uniquely colored eggs. In contrast, under the selective pressure of brood parasitism (the laying of eggs in the nest of another), a bird's reproductive success is enhanced if it can recognize the eggs of other birds in its clutch and then discard them. The possibility of parasitism would place selective pressure on the host bird to detect the odd-colored eggs. This would, in turn, put pressure on the parasite to produce eggs resembling those of its host.

Several species of cuckoo may have evolved the most sophisticated egg-color matching. The European cuckoo, for example, never builds a nest of its own. Among the various birds it victimizes are wagtails, which have white eggs densely spotted with gray; bramblings, whose pale-blue eggs have reddish spots; and European redstarts, which have blue, unspotted eggs. The cuckoo eggs found in these nests usually match closely those of their hosts. The accuracy of the imitations is sometimes so good that even the human eye has difficulty in distinguishing the eggs of the parasite from those of the host.

It was long a mystery how such color matching could occur, for surely cuckoos do not control the pigment glands in their ovaries in order to match their eggs to those of their intended victims. The real answer, however, is almost as bizarre: In any given area, the cuckoos are thought to be made up of reproductively isolated subgroups called "gentes," whose females restrict their parasitism to particular hosts. Two or more gentes may occupy the same area, each parasitizing its own host. A given female always lays eggs of the same color, as will her daughters after her. She must identify the proper host, and this means that an adult female cuckoo will parasitize a bird like her foster parents.

In European passerine birds heavily parasitized by cuckoos, there has been potent selective pressure to foil the parasitism. Hosts have developed a strong attention to the egg color code, abandoning many nests with cuckoo eggs or throwing these eggs out. This puts stronger pressure, on the cuckoos to produce even better egg mimicry. Only the well-matched eggs are accepted, and even then not all of them.

Parasitism in North America is no less severe, but the principal parasite of songbirds, the brown-headed cowbird, thus far has not evolved egg-color mimicry. Nevertheless, the cowbird is a highly successful parasite. It is one of the most common of our native passerine birds, and it is also one of the most widely distributed. According to Herbert

Friedmann, a longtime student of avian brood parasitism, the cowbird—unlike a cuckoo gente, which is restricted to only one or a very few species of hosts—parasitizes more than three hundred and fifty species and subspecies of birds. Some species suffer heavily. Up to 78 percent of all song-sparrow nests in some areas have been victimized by this parasite. The cowbird, however, also occasionally lays eggs in the nests of such unlikely potential hosts as the spotted sandpiper and the ruby-crowned kinglet, where its eggs get damaged or evicted. Thus, there are both advantages and disadvantages to its nonselectivity, but the balance depends on the acceptance behavior of the birds it comes in contact with.

The cowbird was formerly known as the "buffalo bird" and is partial to open habitat. It has spread east from short-grass prairies in the Midwest only within the last two hundred years. In the Midwest, its former range, there is the beginning of color matching between some hosts and the cowbirds' eggs. Apparently some hosts are evolving rejection behavior. But in the East, which the cowbird invaded after the creation of open pastures, it still wreaks havoc among songbirds. In a recent study, Scott K. Robinson, of the Center for Wildlife Ecology, in Illinois, found that 90 percent of ninety-two wood-thrush nests were parasitized with an average of three cowbird eggs.

At this point in the evolutionary race, only some of the potential victims of the brown-headed cowbird have evolved appropriate egg-rejection responses. Stephen I. Rothstein, of the University of California at Santa Barbara, determined this by making plaster-of-Paris eggs and painting them to mimic cowbird eggs. He deposited these in a total of six hundred and forty nests of forty-three species. He found

that two-thirds of the passerine birds accepted the parasite eggs, while only one-fourth consistently rejected them.
Some birds, such as the red-winged blackbird, the yellow
warbler, the phoebe, and the barn swallow, consistently
accepted both fake and real parasite eggs, while others,
such as the catbird, the robin, and the kingbird, consistently rejected them. Since the birds were either consistent
"accepters" or "rejecters," he speculated that once the rejection behavior was genetically coded, it was of such great
advantage that it spread rapidly and became fixed. We usually think of natural selection occurring over eons. Will
wood thrushes and the threatened Kirtland's warbler (which
most authorities believe would be extinct now if it were not
for cowbird-control programs in its breeding area) genetically encode rejection behavior in time and be saved from
extinction? As with all threatened species, a large population
base is necessary for a source of genetic variability to draw
from, but once present, the trait will spread most quickly in
a small population.

Since a key component of defense against parasitism
involves egg recognition, you would predict that means of
detecting foreign eggs would evolve. For example, it would
be easier to recognize a stranger's egg if all one's own eggs
within a clutch were similar. Does this help explain that
songbirds subject to parasitism have *uniform* egg coloring
in the eggs of one clutch, while birds such as hawks, ravens,
and crows, which are not plagued by egg parasites, have a
variety of egg colorations in their clutches?

There are at least three models for a mechanism of rejection behavior. The bird could either innately recognize its
own uniquely colored eggs, or it could innately discriminate

against all "odd" eggs, or it could learn what its first egg looks like (like the murre), and then discriminate against all others. (It would then also have to evolve the behavior to abandon its nest or to remove the offending egg.) The last hypothesis is the most likely. Some sixty years ago, Bernhard Rensch, studying mimicry of cuckoo eggs in Germany, experimented by replacing the first three eggs in a nest of the garden warbler with lesser white-throat eggs. The warbler then ejected its *own* fourth egg! Rensch concluded that egg rejection was not on the basis of recognition of a bird's own eggs but on the basis of the discordance in appearance relative to the other eggs in the nest. But recent experiments by Rothstein show that, like the murres studied by Tschantz, some songbirds also learn to recognize the appearance of their own eggs, becoming imprinted with the image of the first egg they see in the nest. In an experiment that showed this most clearly, Rothstein removed all eggs in a catbird nest each day as they were laid, replacing them with cowbird eggs. Although catbirds normally reject cowbird eggs placed with their own, this catbird accepted a whole clutch of cowbird eggs. When Rothstein added a single catbird egg to the nest with cowbird eggs, the catbird rejected its own egg.

Why don't more birds practice the art of parasitism? As with many historical questions, we don't have an ironclad answer, but we may identify some of the selective processes at work. One possibility is that after a parasite has become established, and through millions of years improved its strategy, the hosts will have such good methods of egg detection that another bird just starting out would have no success. For example, the brown-headed cowbird could not likely become established in Europe, because the European birds, already under selective pressure to detect strange eggs because of the cuckoo, have evolved such a sophisticated egg-recognition system that they would not be fooled by the crude tactics of the cowbird. Analogies with the immune system—or for that matter political systems—come to mind.

There is another important implication of parasitism—one that affects the *variety* of egg colors among species. We can go from the premise that a parasite would have a great advantage if it could utilize a variety of hosts. And multiple parasitism would be easy if all of the parasite's potential victims had similar eggs. Any bird lucky enough to have *distinctively* marked eggs will most easily spot and reject a parasite's eggs. For example, brown-headed cowbird eggs are spotted brown, as are song-sparrow eggs. Song sparrows rarely reject cowbird eggs. But robins and catbirds, both of which have blue eggs, almost always do. Indeed, they reject any egg that contrasts with their own, not just cowbird eggs. For the fun of it, I have for several years painted robins' eggs red, blue, green, and other colors and then replaced them in their nests. The greater the color contrast from their own, the more likely are the robins to reject the "foreign" egg. That is, the robins uniformly throw out red eggs, but they commonly accept green- or blue-painted eggs, which look more like their own. Presumably birds which by chance (random mutation, for example) have purple, green, or pink eggs should also easily become rejectors of white brown-spotted (cowbird) eggs. In other words, to avoid parasitism a bird should have eggs that are different from those whose nests the parasite already uses. This would make for variety of egg color codes among different species but uniformity within the clutches of eggs in a single nest. And in general these are the patterns we see in nature.

Egg parasitism by cowbirds and cuckoos is very costly to the hosts, because the parasite destroys the entire clutch of the host; the young parasite hogs all the food, or pushes the foster parents' babies out of the nest. However, there is another, more subtle parasitism—that of birds laying their eggs in the nests of others of their own kind. For example, Harry Powers, of Rutgers University, has recently found that more than a third of European starling nests may contain at least one parasite egg of the same species, Starlings (which nest in holes) are unable to detect a stranger's eggs, and for "insurance" against such parasitism the birds lay no more than five eggs in a clutch, rather than six. Powers notes that, "If you start with five and pick up a parasite egg, you can handle it, but if you start with six, and get an extra one, you'll fall off the edge, because you won't have the resources to raise the clutch. Then *all* suffer." Chickens also routinely dump their eggs into any chicken nest they find, thus abrogating parental responsibility. Sociobiologist Paul Sherman at Cornell University has noticed such "egg dumping" in wood ducks. The behavior has been most observed in waterbirds under relatively crowded conditions or conditions of limited nest sites. It is probably especially likely in colonial birds and in birds whose eggs are hidden from view. Charles R. Brown, of Yale University, found that cliff swallows regularly deposit their eggs in neighboring nests whenever the opportunity affords. Recently, Charles Trost, of Idaho State University, found eggs of pinyon jays and magpies he had marked in one nest appearing in others of the same species, suggesting that the birds actually carried their own eggs to another nest. Perhaps there is, after all, an evolutionary reason for the "general tendency of birds toward diversity." Catbirds' eggs, by being blue, may be less camouflaged, but they may gain by providing a sharp contrast, so that a parasite's egg can be detected and evicted.

It would be strange indeed if birds had not evolved counterstrategies to reduce this perhaps most pervasive parasitism of all—that of laying eggs in nests of members of one's own species. Egg coloration could again play a major role, as it does in interspecific parasitism. If any individual bird had eggs of a different color from those of its neighbors and potential exploiters, then it would have a means of detecting their deceptions. It cannot mark its own eggs with initials, but unique markings would be equivalent. Few such studies are available, in part because egg collectors were impressed with the astounding differences among species and so collected only one or a very few sets of eggs thought characteristic of a particular species.

But within species, differences exist. Dr. Elsie C. Collias, of the University of California at Los Angeles, has found from a study of over a thousand eggs from thirty-four individuals, of a captive colony of African village weaverbirds that different females consistently laid differently colored eggs. Furthermore, her colleague Dr. J. K. Victoria went on to demonstrate that these females recognize their own eggs, because they reject from their nests those of other females that are marked differently from their own. A recent study by Wendy Jackson at the University of Washington showed that as many as a third of the African weaverbird nests in anyone colony contain a parasite egg from another weaver. But females eject the odd-colored eggs. Presumably a female takes a chance that her egg will match those in another nest. Normally, a weaver can rear only three chicks at a time, so a fourth egg in its own nest is wasted, and the gamble to lay an "extra" egg in another nest has a potential payoff.

It will likely not be possible ever to say with any degree of precision why a robin's egg is blue or a kingbird's egg is white and splotched with dark brown and purple. However, the diversity of patterns shows that: there are different selective pressures at work. The coloration of birds' eggs reflects a long interplay of evolutionary forces, in the face of randomness and chance. This, in turn, "colors" the mind as well as the eye, and gives eggs an additional beauty that no person's brush could ever impart.

BIG BIRD GONE BAD

· · · ·

(CHARLES GRAEBER)

I'VE COME to Australia in search of a giant dinosaur bird called the southern cassowary, but so far all I've found is Bruce: three hundred pounds and twelve fluid ounces of forty-something bearded banana farmer balanced on a bar stool like a fat ballerina and squinting hard at his index finger.

"See, it's the claws you have to look out for," Bruce explains. He draws his finger down his T-shirt, throat to navel. "Like razors. They hook one in you and *splat*!—you're unzipped like a laundry duffel."

Bruce and I are sitting in the El Arish Pub, a living monument to cold beer and bad taxidermy at the edge of Licuala State Forest in Mission Beach, North Queensland, well up Australia's northeast coast. The El Arish is a banana man's grange, a place where plantation laborers pass rainy Sunday afternoons swilling VB stubbies, watching rugby, and swapping stories. With twelve feet (four meters) of rain per year, Mission Beach residents have plenty of talking time. Luckily, the cassowaries that live in the area's jungles are providing plenty to talk about.

In April, a busload of Japanese tourists was held hostage by a hungry adult bird as it head-butted the vehicle's door. In May, rambunctious teenage cassowaries totaled five cars in a hotel parking lot, karate-chopping the hoods. In August, the birds chased a few hikers, forcing the temporary closure of Licuala. Then, in September, at the Australian skydiving championships in nearby Tully, parachuters gawked in amazement as an aggravated cassowary chased a ranger's motorcycle up and down the landing strip, attacking the bike with a five-inch (thirteen-centimeter) talon and slicing the mudguard like a Ginsu through a can.

"Thing is, they're usually shy," explains Bruce. "Except when they eat fermented bush fruit. Then they get drunk, and mean." He signals for another beer. "And, mate, that's where your trouble starts."

Australia is famously full of deadly critters and tall tales, but the southern cassowary is both real and, occasionally, dangerous. *Casuarius casuarius* lives up to forty years, and at over six feet (two meters) and 180 pounds (eighty-two kilograms), it is Australia's largest land animal—a member of the 80-million-year-old ratite family and cousin to extinct giants like the elephant bird of Madagascar and the New Zealand moa. (The only other habitat for the southern cassowary and its two smaller cousins, *Casuarius bennetti* and *Casuarius unappendiculatus,* is the dense jungle of Papua New Guinea.) The cassowary's black, hairlike feathers carpet a body as furry as a sheepdog's, its neck rises from fluorescent crimson to deep blue, and its head is capped with a fin-like helmet of tough, keratinous skin. This assemblage is balanced on two three-foot (one-meter) legs capable of bone-crushing kicks and tipped with three formidable claws: one five-inch (thirteen-centimeter) spike and two short, sharp hooks. And like most birds, the cassowary has a mating call; witnesses compare the male's to the wheezing of an old truck with a sick ignition.

In short, the cassowary is hard to miss. The reason I haven't seen one—the reason most people have never even heard of such a bird—is that cassowaries are also rare, and getting rarer. Down from an estimated population of 2,500 in 1988, there are just 1,200 birds today. In 1999, the southern cassowary officially became an endangered species.

"If you do see one," Bruce says, straightening on his stool, "don't turn your back. And don't run—they hate joggers. The pounding of feet triggers fight-or-flight in them, and they don't fly..."

"Hold on," I say. "You're honestly telling me that if I come across a giant, drunken dinosaur with razor claws and a battering-ram helmet, I should stand my ground?"

Bruce drains his beer and motions beyond the saloon doors, where the jungle howls with rain. "If you don't believe me, mate," he says, "head out there and see for yourself."

AROUND MISSION Beach, "out there" is the North Queensland Wet Tropics—a 264-mile (425-kilometer)-long sliver of 100-million-BC jungle running south from Cooktown to Townsville. This particular patch of green is the oldest jungle on the planet, pre-dating the extinction of the dinosaurs by 35 million years. The cassowary evolved amid the Wet Tropics, thriving on figs, quandongs, and other distinctive fruits. Unfortunately, this area is choice habitat for humans, too. And when humans and giant birds share the same real estate, sooner or later they're going to clash.

No comprehensive data on cassowary attacks exists, but it's possible to make estimates. In 1999, Christopher P. Kofron, a ranger for the Queensland Parks and Wildlife Service, compiled a list of 221 attacks reported since the mid-1800s. Scattered among the lists of people chased, charged, kicked, pushed, pecked, jumped on, and headbutted are some serious injuries. The only death—that of a sixteen-year-old hunter named Phillip McClean, who caught a claw to the jugular—occurred more than seventy-five years ago.

Most cassowary crimes are misdemeanors. Typical was the assault on Doon McColl. In April of 1995, Doon was jogging through Mount Whitfield, a park two hours north of Mission Beach, when she heard a noise on the trail behind her.

"I turned and saw this huge black beast," she tells me. "And I just thought, Oh, fuck." Doon ran, then climbed a tree. The bird waited below, pecking furiously at its own neck. Hours later, it finally wandered away.

The very next week, Doon's boyfriend, Ray Willetts, was chased through Mount Whitfield. He tried to lose the bird in the jungle and spent the day flailing through thorns and lawyer vines while the cassowary trotted effortlessly behind. "He came home crosshatched and bleeding and like, 'My God, Doon, it was Jurassic Park!'" Doon recalls.

With millions of acres of wide-open spaces, it's hard to imagine Australia having suburban-sprawl issues. But along the highly coveted tropical northeast coast, one of the country's fastest-growing regions, forest is being razed at an average of 16,549 acres (6,697 hectares) per year, and more than 370,000 people live within twenty miles (thirty-two kilometers) of cassowary habitat.

"When you fragment the cassowary's environment, it's basically a death sentence for them," says George Mansford, the 68-year-old chair of the Australian Rainforest Foundation, a nonprofit conservation group. "The remaining bird populations are concentrated in just a few islands of rainforest connected to one another by thin corridors of jungle. When you cut these corridors with house lots and highways, you have problems. And that's exactly what finally happened at Mount Whitfield."

Mount Whitfield is an island of rainforest surrounded by sprawl from the booming 130,000-person coastal city of Cairns. Its 741 acres (three hundred hectares) are sandwiched between the airport, several housing developments, and the Captain Cook Highway.

Ten years ago, this was the epicenter of cassowary attacks, and today the Mount Whitfield trailhead still bears a menacing NO JOGGING sign. But these days, a three-hour trot here will yield nothing more terrifying than a bush turkey. In 1996, Cairns's last cassowary, a thirty-year-old female locals called Blue Arrow, met her fate in a suburban backyard.

Cassowaries are experts at gutting dogs, and Blue Arrow was no exception. In fact, the old girl was successfully moving in on two bull terriers when 73-year-old Jim Barry tried to pull the dogs away; instead he ended up knocking the big bird off her feet, and off her game. The cassowary managed one last kick—sending Jim flying into an adjacent vegetable patch—before the dogs took her throat.

"And that's the pattern," says Mansford. "Habitat fragmentation, human interaction, dead birds. I don't want the next generation of Australians to have to visit museums to see one. But unless we change the way we think about development in this country, the cassowary is doomed."

THESE DAYS, when a bird gets mauled by dogs or hit by a car, they call Cameron Allanson, 41, the ranger in charge of the Mission Beach Management Unit, which oversees five national parks in prime cassowary territory. In the battle to keep Mission Beach from becoming another Cairns, Ranger Cameron is a frontline foot soldier.

The Mission Beach cassowary population is down from roughly seventy adults in 2000 to approximately forty today, making it the most vulnerable in Queensland. Driving around, it's easy to see why. Mission Beach is a sleepy town smack-dab between the Gondwana rainforest and the white-sand beaches of the Coral Sea, and, as with the Cairns of twenty years ago, both birds and people want to live there.

Today is Cameron's day off, and he's keen to spend it with his wife, Shayne, puttering around their shaded porch with a refrigerator full of cozy-wrapped beers and a fresh pack of rollie ciggies. Like many houses in the Wet Tropics, theirs is on a small lot backing directly onto the rainforest, only a few miles north of town. It features a sort of exposed basement equipped with laundry room, office, and cold-storage freezer. In this case, the freezer does not store hamburger.

In the past four months, Cameron's jurisdiction alone has lost four birds to car accidents. To keep the cassowaries from crossing the road, a 165-mile (266-kilometers) "cassowary corridor" has been proposed, and the town council has launched an awareness campaign for local drivers. Until the speed bumps and CAUTION: CASSOWARY signs kick in, more cassowaries are likely to succumb to traffic, and then the big freezer, where Cameron keeps cassowary roadkill until it can be shipped to the Atherton University biology department in Cairns for study.

"Ah, mate," Cameron says, pulling back the thick black plastic to expose a frozen bird's ankle, thick as a wrist. "So many things you don't know when you first start a job like this. Like when you pick up the dead bird, you have to fold it up before it gets rigor mortis. When it stretches out hard at its full size, it won't fit."

According to Cameron, the birds do actually seem to dislike joggers. He's watched more than one Lycra-clad tourist go screaming down the road, Walkman flailing, cassowary in pursuit. Still, he reckons that most attacks aren't motivated by a hatred of Reeboks but by something simpler: food and sex.

The food issue is familiar. Park animals start associating people with food, and the next thing you know, it's your sandwich or your life. The sex issue is more complex. While the female birds roam the jungle during the months of May and June (the only time of year they'll tolerate a male's presence) on their annual sex bender, males stay put for up to fifty days, protecting the three to five giant, pale-green eggs the female lays and then tending to the chicks. Perhaps it's this arrangement that makes male cassowaries a bit touchy about sharing turf. Every mating season, Cameron sees it all: jealous males kicking out their reflections in car doors and windows, or disoriented and walking into, well, everywhere—pubs, houses, churches, and, increasingly, roads.

Last season, at a four-star luxury retreat in Cairns, a brood of adolescent cassowaries found its way to the hotel's pool. One of the birds snatched a purse off a bikinied tanner's chaise lounge. For the next ten minutes, the guests were treated to the sight of a grown man in a Speedo chasing the big bird round and round the patio. Finally the cassowary lost its footing on the slick Mexican tile and skated hard into the lunch buffet. Apparently, at that point, it dropped the purse.

BEFORE CAMERON and Shayne started this job, their house was owned by an old German couple named Frieda and Joseph Jorissen. They made a fair go growing lemons, mandarins, and oranges, but mostly they tended the birds, and over their 42-year tenure in Mission Beach, Frieda became the grande dame of cassowary culture. In 1977, the Jorissens donated the property to the National Parks and Wildlife Services and, by extension, to Cameron and Shayne. Little did they know that the deal came with a history, and a price.

"Basically, there were generations of birds who had grown up getting handouts off this veranda," says Cameron. "And, mate, they were more than a little upset when we put up the fence."

One giant female paced a deep trench around the perimeter. Others harassed their car when they came back from the grocery store, pecking the glass, scaring the kids, chasing the dog, making life hell.

"I tell you, it was a bit of a pissing contest at first, but we've got an understanding now," he says, outlining a complex "understanding" program involving trash-can lids.

"Bird!" cries Shayne. She's been out back, examining a giant python that has eaten a neighbor's cat—you can still see the kitty's pricked ears through the snake's skin—and has spotted a 150-pound (sixty-eight-kilogram), six-foot-tall (two-meter) female.

I push up from the picnic table for a glimpse. And, yes, there is something in the woods over Cameron's shoulder, a spot of red. Then a head, or what looks like a head, sticking out from the jungle like a sock puppet through a stage curtain. Then it pulls back, lost in the bush.

"Did you see her?" asks Cameron, cracking me another beer.

I have to admit: I'm really not sure.

BEFORE I leave, Cameron offers two more beers, and two suggestions on where to actually spot a cassowary.

"Well, you can go right on out across the road there," he says, pointing to the end of their lot. "That's all lowland rainforest, right to the coast. Walk there, down to the swamps, and you'll get a real taste for it, all right. You know how to handle leeches, I reckon?"

This option is appealing, but since cassowaries, like people, prefer paths to thickets, the odds of buttonholing a bird in the bush are vanishingly small. I choose instead a flat six-mile (ten-kilometer) track traversing Licuala State Forest Park, where the giant fan palms and prehistoric cycad trees start a few feet from the parking lot.

Enormous trees breach the canopy. Rain roars against the leaves and pools in muddy pits tusked by feral pigs, and the air carries a spunky, living scent. Sometimes there's a rustling in the bush, but each time I turn, nothing's there. And frankly, at this point, I'm not sure I want anything to be.

It's then that I realize that the black shape walking toward me is not a hiker. At twenty feet (six meters), it's moving forward in the deliberate manner of movie monsters.

At fifteen feet (4.5 meters), the colors on its neck are vivid and neon, its head is capped by a casque of lopsided bone, its glossy black body sprouts a foliage of quills. It picks up each giant foot and places it delicately ahead, first one, then the other, like a huge marionette. Ten feet (three meters) now, then five (1.5 meters), and the cassowary stops to regard me sideways, the velociraptor equivalent of the hairy eyeball. Is it angry, drunk, mean? Is it surprised? Hungry?

The questions stop as it again moves toward me, this time faster. Forget the theories; it's time to walk. Backward. Slowly. I keep the distance, remembering the pecked and chased and butted.

"Don't dare run," Bruce had suggested. "And never turn your back on a bird." But, really, how could anyone turn away? The cassowary pecks the ground, gobbling fat worms with quick chops of its beak. Its legs are turquoise and muscular, its wedge toes are finished with those famous curved razors of spike and claw, and I have no idea what to do. Look for a tree? Suddenly they all seem desperately flimsy for the job. Run? Not on your life.

Instead, I take one deliberate step to the side, offering the cassowary the trail. The bird cocks its head, then struts past. It is real. Then, just as quickly, it is gone.

MINUS ONE

· · · ·

(DAN KOEPPEL)

LIKE A bird hiding in thick forest, Dad's avian desires
emerged for brief periods throughout his life, offering
a seductive glimpse, then vanishing, leaving nothing but the
faint and fading rustle of feathers; it was a siren, promising
to add meaning to his life, but never solidly enough for him
to truly embrace—though with each departure, it left stronger and stronger longings. After his divorce, Dad's birding
self barely surfaced; it was as if his two sides had chosen to
live entirely separate lives, and if they passed each other as
they made their way to their destination—the sighting of a
rare duck on the way out to a singles house Dad shared in
the Hamptons—they were scarcely acknowledged.

In fact, there was very little birding at all. Dad lived just
a block from Central Park, and sometimes he'd quit work

early and scan the meadows and glades with his binoculars. Nothing new. His New York list was full enough that adding something novel to it was less a matter of chance than attentiveness, as with the Saw-whet Owl, which he'd been told about, then sought.

There were other distractions. Though Dad had an active dossier of singles-bar encounters, he also had two children to support, the still-fresh wounds of divorce to tend to, and pressing financial needs. When I asked Dad if the split might have led to an embrace of opportunity, the chance to rededicate his life to birds, he said, "I was almost broke, and I had to concentrate on getting my life started." Once again, Dad chose normalcy, responsibility, and—at that point—the best facsimile of the life his parents had wanted for him over whatever personal ambitions he might have harbored.

The free-spirited pleasures of that era seemed to take the edge off Dad's loneliness and heartbreak. But on the rare occasions on which birds did reveal themselves to him, Dad was faced with his own deeper identity. Those moments exposed his true frustrations because they were more than just gratifying—they were gorgeous; they were transcendent; they were fleeting glimpses of a different, secret self. But I think Dad knew that to embrace birding completely would mean a life of far greater solitude. He was compelled to bird, but less obsessed with it, at least at that point in his life. And as more and more of his friends got divorced and joined the same permissive scene he was part of, the oddity and heartbreak of his broken family seemed less shameful, less anomalous. In other words, the definition of a "normal" life had caught up with the events that had, not so much earlier, made him feel completely isolated. Being divorced in Manhattan wasn't what he'd originally wanted, but it was fun, and he was no longer alone at it. The space the birding filled in him had, because of circumstance, briefly shrunk.

. . .

NUMERIC LANDMARKS—THE five hundredth species, or checking off every bird known to occur in your state—are the key snapshots of birding progress. But there are also more organic thresholds, places where a birder graduates to a higher level of the activity. Often, moving up that notch plants the seeds that ultimately bloom into competitive birding, into the need to see everything. For nearly every Big Lister I've met, the most important of these soft boundaries, the one that lights the spark of competitiveness and obsession, is a first-time visit to the tropics. The reason is simple: more birds.

There are about eight hundred bird species found in the United States. Seeing them all is a huge goal, and one that many listers spend years trying to achieve; there's a subgroup of competitive birders who try to see as many of these species as they can in a single year. (Field-guide author Kenn Kaufman shattered the "Big Year" record in 1973, seeing 671 species; he was nineteen years old and broke, and undertook the adventure with little more than the clothes on his back, a pair of binoculars, and an uncanny ability to hitch rides almost anywhere.) But even for these breakneck birders, a first visit to the world's equatorial regions is an exercise in ornithological ecstasy. Such an excursion can yield hundreds of new species; a moderately experienced U.S. birder might double a list he or she had taken years to build in just the first few days of a trip to Brazil or Peru.

Even less-formidable tropical destinations, like the Caribbean, are riotously rich in avifauna, and often act as triggers for birders who have had deeply buried grand ambitions.

. . .

IF IT was a "whim," as Dad says, it was an impromptu moment a long time in the making. After two years of what Dad characterizes as "infrequent and nonproductive bird-ing"—no new species—in early 1973, he set off on his own brief adventure. He'd been scheduled as a drug lecturer on an educational cruise for doctors, but arrived at the ship's originating port in Montego Bay, Jamaica, three days early. He rented a car and drove into the mountains above Kingston.

It was a magnificent afternoon, sunny and tranquil. He spotted fifteen new birds, and fun ones, in quick succession. It felt nearly intoxicating. The other appeal of the tropics is that the avifauna are much more distinctive there than in temperate zones (more species, evolved to fill more niches, some biologists believe). The next day, he drove into a misty valley called Hardwar Gap; he'd been told about it by some of the New York birders with whom he kept in touch. It was Dad's first experience in true jungle: dark, wet woods, birds everywhere, but the thick vegetation made it truly chal-lenging to see them. Dad added three to his list, though he missed the difficult-to-spot Jamaican Blackbird. "The Blue Mountains were just fascinating," Dad says. "I was completely amazed at how dense and beautiful they were."

(Nearly every other birder I've spoken to describes a similar fascination with an inaugural tropical visit; as an outdoors writer, I experienced this myself on my first trip to such a climate, when I biked to the steamy bottom of Mexico's Copper Canyon. Between the wild macaws and papayas growing from trees, I decided that I'd found paradise; I've since visited the spot on eight separate occasions, and I can't wait to go back.)

The day before the cruise began, Dad visited one of this hemisphere's most lush birding spots. The Rocklands Hummingbird Sanctuary sits a mile (about one-and-a-half kilometers) up a muddy dirt road, but the journey—then and today—remains one of the Caribbean's most worthwhile and lovely nature pilgrimages. The tiniest birds on earth flit above a roughly manicured garden, usually as a few hardy tourists gawk. The refuge was the domain of an early ornithological eccentric: Lisa Salmon—known to the locals as "Miss Lisa"—served in the Women's Royal Air Force during World War II; upon cessation of hostilities, she built a small home in the hills and thereafter spent most of her time scolding and charming anyone in a position to advance bird conservation. By the 1950s, her hummingbird feedings, held at precisely 3:15 every afternoon, became a mandatory stopover for birders looking to see hard-to-find species like the dark purple Jamaican Mango and the outlandish Red-billed Streamertail, with its multicolored beak and a pair of bannerlike tail feathers that stretch back up to twelve inches (thirty centimeters). Salmon showed both species to my dad, who was by then in a minor overture to the listing frenzy that would fully overtake him a few years later. He nearly missed the cruise ship, boarding just before it departed Montego Bay,

thrilled to have expanded his life list by thirty-eight birds—
his biggest single haul since he was a teenager.

. . .

ON THE boat trip, Dad veered between his post-divorce
distractions and his reawakened interest in counting birds.
He hooked up with the cruise ship's Swedish hostess;[1] the
fling, he says, was light entertainment, though there was
one moment in his recollection, that was subtly telling, that
speaks of the sense of isolation always so close to him, yet
always keeping so much at bay. Dad had become friends
with another lecturer; a psychologist who'd found his own
hostess girlfriend onboard. One evening, as the ship cruised
toward port in Cartagena, Colombia, the two men stood on
deck—Dad had his binoculars, of course—and celebrated
their good fortune.

"Richard," the psychologist said, with a quick intimacy
that hinted at the long friendship that would follow, "I'm in
love."[2]

---

1 The girl's name was a sexually suggestive double entendre, similar to the "Pussy
Galore" character found in the James Bond movie *Goldfinger*. I found this amusing,
in an obscure way, since it hints at the genuine connection the British spy hero has
with birding. Novelist Ian Fleming was an avid lister and lived in Jamaica on an
estate called "Goldeneye" (named after a species of duck). When he was trying to
name the hero of his soon-to-be-famous series of thrillers, his eye wandered to his
own bookshelf, where he saw the same bird guide Dad used for his Jamaican trip.
Finding the author's name to be suitably "dull and anonymous," he appropriated it
for secret agent 007; in Dad's later birding career, his frequent absences prompted
some local speculation that he was himself a spy, a perception Dad, if not encour-
aging it, found amusing.

2 Their friendship was ended by Arthur's untimely suicide in the early 1990s. That—
and the early loss of another close friend—gave Dad, as he says, "even less to do at
home," and more reasons to go out birding.

"You're not in love," Dad replied curtly. "You've been smoking too much dope." The drug lecturers took a position that was common in those days—that marijuana was generally not harmful, and certainly less of a danger than alcohol.)

"Yes, I am," said the psychologist.

"No," said Dad, ever rational. "You've just taken all your needs and desires and projected them onto this woman."

The shrink stared toward the lights of the South American city they were approaching. "Isn't that what love is?" he replied.

Dad didn't have an answer; his needs and desires, his love wasn't about a relationship. At least, not with a person.

.   .   .

I ALSO felt alone. I was eleven years old and just entering junior high school. My father was mostly absent, and my mother, who was present, didn't seem to want to be there. I spent most of my time by myself; I'd pedal my bike to the edge of Little Neck Bay, and I'd sit there, looking at the birds, but also at the bridges and cars, at the boats, and especially at the airplanes (we were in the flight path of LaGuardia Airport) taking off for distant places. The anger and tension that had overwhelmed my parents' marriage hadn't vanished—Mom and Dad were still fighting, post-divorce, usually over money—and it made me feel like a surrogate for Dad on Ridge Road, which was becoming a more and more bizarre place to live: Our house was always overloaded with people, sounds, and smells. I felt completely ignored and sometimes threatened by Mom's friends. My biggest relationships were with the equally alienated children of my mother's other few divorced friends, but even seeing them was rare.

Like Dad when he was my age, I needed to escape. Also like him, I got on my bike and pedaled to the marshes. But I never saw a Brown Thrasher. Nothing that was outside of me caught my interest and transported me to emotional safety, or, as my mother invited a parade of strangers—some of whom decided they had the right to discipline Jim and me as they saw fit—into our home, to physical safety. I ultimately found my refuge: I dwelled more and more in fantasy, located somewhere between a tropical paradise under the North Pole (as in one of my favorite books of that time, Edgar Rice Burroughs's *At the Earth's Core*) and a perfect future, where misfit teens were bestowed with commissions aboard the starship *Enterprise*.

Unlike my father's, my obsessions didn't involve soaring, but vanishing into those worlds. In order to encourage my reading, Dad came up with what we called "The Deal": Anytime I'd finish a book, he'd buy me another. I collected authors serially, reading all ninety-six of Lester Dent's "Doc Savage" pulp novels, in order; the entire twenty-six volume Tarzan series; all of Kurt Vonnegut's published work (at the time, seven books) in chronological order; and both *The Iliad* and *The Odyssey*. I was an avid comic-book collector—it was my own form of listing, and each of my titles was as perfectly logged, categorized, and cross-referenced as any bird on Dad's tally. I had to buy every single comic that hit the news-stand on Tuesdays, when the new shipments would arrive. It didn't matter whether it was *Spider-Man, Casper the Friendly Ghost,* or some romance cartoon aimed at girls. My goal as a collector was completeness, and order. Dad encouraged this minor duplication of his own personality; when the Scholastic Book Club issued its quarterly catalog for student purchases, he'd allow me to order every single one, as long as I promised to read them all. I'd arrange the new volumes in alphabetical order and plow through them, one at a time, never varying, and I finished each and every one—even if I didn't like the book.

·   ·   ·

WHEN THE cruise ship docked at Cartagena, Dad took a quick break along the shoreline. Today, bird scientists have traipsed to every end of South America, producing elaborate field guides that list most of the continent's more than four thousand species. But then, the author of one of the very first of those guides—Steve Hilty, whose *A Guide to the Birds of Colombia* was published in 1986—had only just arrived in that country as a twenty-two-year-old Peace Corps volunteer. Over the next decade, Hilty and his collaborator, William Brown, would catalog the birds they encountered, sending their descriptions back to Guy Tudor—an American bird artist whose style is reminiscent of Peterson's, though slightly more lush and painterly—and ultimately producing over 1,700 listings for that reference. But no such book existed in the early 1970s. Whether hobbyist or professional, visitors to places with lots of birds arrived with little information on what—or where—they were. So, departing the boat, Dad took a simple approach. He hailed a cab and told the driver to take him "to the nearest swamp." Fifteen minutes later, eleven new birds were on his list—including the Wattled Jacana, a tallish bird with elongated toes that, similar to a daddy longlegs, have evolved to allow it to walk gracefully on floating vegetation. The next day, the boat headed through the Panama Canal, with another brief stop.

Dad had gotten directions to a birding location from a friend in New York, but was unable to locate the exact area. It didn't matter. "There were birds everywhere," Dad says. "It felt so good to be alone, enjoying myself, with nothing to worry about." It was as if he were in an over-humid version of Flushing Meadows, living the life he'd put off for so long. In a single afternoon, he matched his three-day Jamaican total. The thirty-eight species he added made the Panama stopover his biggest day ever.

The boat continued on to St. Andrew Islands, Guatemala, and finally to Cozumel, Mexico. He added a dozen more new birds, for a life list total of 834. This was a birder who was beginning to become well-traveled. An idea was forming: "It was very exciting to go someplace and be surrounded by nothing but new birds." On the flight home, he began to think about other places that had lots of new birds: Trinidad. Kenya. Brazil. How many birds were there to see? An answer, for Dad, was beginning to form.

All of them.

· · ·

I LOVED the way birds made Dad an expert in something. His ability to identify what was floating overhead from just a quick glance seemed like a superpower, on par with the skills my comic-book idols possessed. But I didn't really like birds myself. I tried. I had my binoculars and my field guide; I had the Bayside Woods within throwing distance of my house. But I just didn't think they were interesting, and I was getting past the age—about ten or eleven—where most kids get hooked on birds. I'd already found my refuge. I think the difference was that Dad's birding grew as an escape from a place that was cold, from the Spartan and serious environment that Rose and Morris created. My refuge needed to take me from a far hotter place; escaping the chaos of living in Douglaston required distant fantasy worlds, places I never really had to depart, and which could never be destroyed.

But the one time Dad's birding did rub off on me made me feel so proud of him and of being his son. The autumn after Dad's cruise, an elderly man visited P.S. 98, the tiny elementary school near the Douglaston train station, to talk to us about nature, and about birds in particular. He had two methods of inciting interest in kids who were probably more interested in sports or watching television: First, he carried with him an impressively huge, taxidermied barn owl; second, he had a game to play.

"Who thinks they know a lot about birds?" Will Astle asked.

Hands shot up, but mine wasn't among them. Astle refined his question: "Can any of you name ten different kinds of bird?"

Again a few hands shot up, and the visitor called on them one by one.

Robin . . . bluebird . . . cardinal . . . chicken?

The next kid added "sea gull."

I knew *sea gull* was a generic term, and therefore wrong, and that chicken—well, that just didn't count because they were talking about the kind your grandmother made into soup, and it was beneath mentioning. Still, I hadn't raised my hand. I was too scared to speak. Mr. Astle asked again, and again.

Finally, I knew I had to volunteer. I could tell by the look on his face that he expected me to falter, as the other boys did.

It wasn't easy. I wasn't used to being under pressure, and I kept drawing blanks. Cardinal. Robin. Starling. Bald eagle.

Those were the obvious ones.

Barn swallow.

I paused, but Astle gave me time.

Herring gull.

He raised his eyebrows.

Osprey. Saw-whet Owl.

All birds Dad had shown me.

One more. Again, I drew a blank—and then, of course, it was there. How could I forget the two most important birds? Jim's favorite, and mine.

Hoopoe. Scissor-tailed Flycatcher.

Mr. Astle's eyes lit up. I had named one bird that wasn't even found on the continent, and another that was only seen in Texas. My teacher, Mrs. Quinn, applauded, and the rest of the class was duly impressed. But Astle was the happiest. Birding, as I've said, appeals especially to young boys— maybe because it adds a very rational, linear structure to adventure. Astle's purpose in going to schools, I later learned, wasn't just to get a bunch of blasé kids slightly pumped up about nature; it was to find young potential birders and steer them onto the right path.

Will Astle believed he'd found one that day.

"What's your name?" he asked.

"Danny," I replied. "Danny Koeppel."

He smiled. "Ahh," he said, "you must be Richard's son."

It turned out that, in his early teens, Dad had seen the very same stuffed owl; Will Astle was one of the founders of the Queens County Bird Club. After class, Mr. Astle asked me if I knew any other kids who liked birds. I didn't, and he was slightly disappointed that he hadn't found an untouched prodigy (since it was assumed that my birding education was in good hands). Still, he was relieved to assume—though it wouldn't turn out to be true, either for Jim or for me—that P.S. 98 would be well represented by at least one junior avian enthusiast.

. . .

THERE'S AN irony to listing: The more birds you count, the more you leave the world of flesh and feather and enter a universe of abstractions, of human-imposed taxonomic decisions that can change your tally, even if you're just sitting at home. At the end of 1973, the American Ornithologists' Union announced the lumping of the Blue Goose with the Snow Goose, and the Eurasian and Green-Winged Teal. There was also a split between the Willow and Alder Flycatchers. Most birders never experience (or at least aren't terribly aware of) such technical fluctuations in their list, and though Dad's net loss was just a single bird, it would be the beginning of a decade of huge changes in the way birds were defined (and counted), ultimately leading to a statistical end to most lumping, and an explosion in the number of split species. Dad found the reduction of his total, tiny as it was, disconcerting: "I can't say why," says dad, "but it felt strange." My guess is that it violated the sense of order that his birding most indulged. A seemingly inexplicable and surprising change in his list added uncertainty to the thing that had always been his rock. (He'd later come to fully embrace those uncertainties, especially after he saw how they could be studied and exploited to build his numbers, and therefore his ultimate sense of control.)

CALL *and* RESPONSE

. . . .

(SUSAN CERULEAN)

WORDS ARE what I do for a living, but I do not trust them entirely. They do not generally sink to the bone. They can be retracted. In my job at the state wildlife conservation agency, I sometimes witnessed the rewriting of truth by editing or by excision. Example: I was assigned to write a five-hundred-word piece on the natural history of the whooping crane for a Florida lifestyle magazine. I listed the things that have led to the bird's extreme endangerment, and one of these threats was hunting. Deliberate shooting. Hot bullets hurtling into flesh and feathers. I didn't put it that graphically, of course. I simply wrote: "Habitat loss and illegal hunting were among the causes of this crane's decline."

A supervisor one hopscotch above me in the agency chain of command handed me back the story draft: "Take out the part about hunting," he said.

"Why?" I asked, horrified. "That's what happened! It was true!"

"It will just upset our constituents," he said. "We don't need to go there. It doesn't happen anymore."

Before he would allow the story to go forward, he required me to backspace that phrase, those true words, right off the page. As if it never happened. In this way, we rewrote history, made it prettier and more palatable, just a little bit of it, just a little at a time. And supposedly that was okay because our agency is the powerful ally of wildlife, its primary advocate in our state, the place where the best resources are centered.

But it makes me wonder, What else has not been said?

What if you are only told part of the truth? What if I know something essential and I withhold it from you because it is so painful?

Sometimes scientists are fabulous storytellers; Ken Meyer is one of them. I've wondered: If these experts are willing to tell all they know, as Ken does, aren't their words enough to see to the planet's conservation, and swallow-tailed kites specifically? The biologists I know are articulate and airtight and can be passionate, even, as they report their findings. And since they are the experts, what is my role? Especially if I am not willing to restrict myself to merely reporting what others have learned? I suspect there is more to the truth, to world-changing truth telling, than the unadorned facts of science, important as they are.

ABOUT EIGHT years ago, I was invited along with twenty-five other environmentalists to meet with Florida's lieutenant governor in rare, intimate conversation. We gathered in a circle in the plush living room of a remote ranch house near Ocala, speaking in turn on behalf of our organizations: Sierra, Audubon, Friends of the Everglades, the Nature Conservancy, 1000 Friends of Florida, others. My colleagues asked the lieutenant governor to speed the Everglades cleanup, fund more land acquisition, do more for energy conservation. Everyone was so eloquent, full of facts, advocating like the lawyers many of them were. My turn drew closer; I didn't have any planned remarks. My heart raced; I felt myself shivering. All I could think about were kites.

And so I launched into an unrehearsed description of the plight of swallow-tailed kites in Florida. I described the vulnerable roost, the graceful birds, my desire for my young son to be able to see them all his life, and for all Florida's children to know and revere them. My eyes shone with hot tears. I had no hard data or solutions to offer. My throat closed; I stopped. The lieutenant governor responded to me, kindly, vaguely. No one else spoke. The woman next to me picked up the Everglades legal suit as if I had never spoken. I averted my gaze, hugged my knees, felt like a fool. I had violated an unspoken rule of this political setting. I had exposed my heart.

I gazed out the plate-glass windows, wondering if I would ever be an effective advocate if I couldn't keep my emotions under wraps. Or if I'd ever want to. As I sagged into the misery of my thoughts, a swallow-tailed kite arced into view, alive, glinting white against the blue sky, just outside the window glass. It shouldn't be here now, I thought to myself. The others of its kind are all at the Okeechobee roost, readying to set out across the gulf for South America.

I caught the eye of a friend; he winked, smiled. I settled back into my body. The others talked on.

THE WRITER Muriel Rukeyser describes two kinds of poetry: the poetry of "unverifiable fact"—that which emerges from dreams, sexuality, subjectivity; and the poetry of "documentary fact"—literally, accounts of strikes, wars, geographical and geological details, actions of actual persons in history, scientific invention. Our culture is most comfortable with documentary fact, the truth of the scientists and academics. What I notice is how split apart are these two ways of knowing truth. One embodied. The other, generally not.

By paying attention to my body, I am learning to feel my way into truth. Just as the rivers are truths carved into the body of the planet, undeniable channels, so we may allow ourselves to fall into the larger body of the earth, rather than the surficial currents and tinny voices of the dominant culture. In the river, the water is tannic and dark, and we cannot see our way to the bottom. We may collide with hard cypress knees or scrape our feet on the lime rock bottom, which is bedrock, what we seek.

One time a swallow-tailed kite, strung taut on its light bones, swooped above me, a pair of kingbirds in close chase. The kite powered fast into the canopy of a spreading live oak, but not before I glimpsed the nestling gripped in its talons. I had forgotten that side of my long-winged birds, how they rip young birds from their nests and eat them raw, floating on the slight breath of the wind.

I ORGANIZED an expedition to Tall Timbers Research Station about thirty miles (forty kilometers) north to look for yellow-breasted chats with my friend, ornithologist Todd Engstrom. The trip was a birthday present for another bird-loving nephew, Garrett, who, with my son, David, hoped to add this secretive warbler to his life list of birds. As we moved slowly through the old pines, easing toward the brushy habitat preferred by chats, Todd quizzed us, tuning up our ears—the voices of birds coupled with a practiced ear are generally the best tools for identifying them in the field. All around us birdsong poured down from the sky.

"Parula warbler," we named. "And pine warbler, great crested flycatcher, red-bellied woodpecker. Northern bob-white."

"What about that one?" he asked, gesturing toward a two-phrased singing.

"Yellow-throated vireo," said my nephew Garrett, quickly, while my own brain shuffled through image and song more slowly.

"Good," said Todd, smiling.

We climbed out of the truck, and where Todd stood became the center, as if at the heart of a compass, his arms the connections between hidden bird and human knowing. He stood at the heart of all that a lifetime of paying close attention in the woods had brought him, the knowledge of each avian voice, without hesitation.

"Indigo bunting." Right arm toward the west, paired notes, long phrasing. "Blue grosbeak."

A slurred *pee-a-weee*: "Eastern wood-pewee."

"Ground dove." Different from the common mourning dove, a single, distinct *coo*.

Each song I have learned before. Some I hear only once a year, some daily. The neurons linking memory and name fire quickly or slowly, depending on intimacy, mine, with each bird's call.

"Yellow-breasted chat!" Todd signaled. There it was, the boys were happy, plunging off into the brush to see the bird, for that is how they love to keep their lists. For them, the sighting means almost everything; for me it is habitat and voice.

"Orchard oriole," says Todd, arm directed high, east. I do not even pick out the notes from the rest at all.

"Where, where?" I ask, frantic to keep up.

We wait, listening.

There, he says again, chopping his extended arm more precisely in the direction of the bird's singing.

I'm frustrated at how barely the oriole's song registers in my brain. It's a different kind of not hearing. I am willing, even eager, to hear the bird and memorize its notes so I'll know in the future when I'm near it, but I am so unpracticed with its sound.

Do you see the danger of this kind of ignorance? If I cannot hear the bird and don't see it, it doesn't exist. Nor might its precise habitat, the things it requires to live. The bird must sing. We must hear it call. Then we must be able to name the animal and what it needs. Then it is time for our voices. Our responding. Our protection of these lives.

The call notes of the birds and their songs go out into the silence, and on the other side of their rattle or scream or song is the same absence of sound. But is it really the same? Is anything changed for the sounding? Do the actual waves of sound that reach my eardrums change anything in any way? Probably birdsong often does induce or suggest movement by others of their kind: I am here. I am foraging. I am looking for a mate. I am a good provider. I have an excellent nest site. There is a predator nearby. I am alive, I am here, I exist. In the swamp forest among the lifting trunks of trees, under the gray sky, the landscape shivers with the circling call of the red-shouldered hawk. Perhaps in some way the rolling waves of sound of the wild things move against one another physically, even at some level contributing to the upholding of trunks, the stance of tall grasses, a counteractive force against gravity. Perhaps voice is a physical part of the matrix of things.

The loss of each species, the muting of any one voice, creates a hole in infinity, limits earth's possibilities. The point of speaking about truth is this: we have a real world, and too much of it is really dying. One of the most captivating aspects of the history of the European settlement of North America is the establishment of democracy, implying a voice for all, as well as a broader tolerance than the monarchies across the Atlantic allowed. But in fact there was a much broader pluralism on this continent before colonization.

We have had to order our lives around denial of this truth, or we couldn't go on in our daily lives as we do. Thirty thousand species, thirty thousand different kinds of lives and voices are wiped from the planet by our excesses and ignorance each year. By our belief that our needs and hungers are greater than the rest of the planet.

But we are also acquainted with the power of voice for the good: how Rachel Carson chose to use that sense of hearing in titling her book *Silent Spring,* thus alerting us to the terrible legacy of pesticides in the 1960s. It's clear that those of us who can raise our heads above denial, and the diversions of the popular culture and our own hopelessness, need to use every variation on voice we have at our disposal to bring the rest of us along: describe and alert and growl and chant and pray. Croon and Whisper and extol and harmonize. Adore and alarm and mourn and insist.

CYCLES IN
THE AIR

WIND BIRDS
Mudflats and Shorebird Migration

. . . .

(DAVID PITT-BROOKE)

The restlessness of shorebirds, their kinship with the distance and swift seasons, the wistful signal of their voices down the long coastlines of the world make them, for me, the most affecting of wild creatures. I think of them as birds of wind, as "wind birds."

PETER MATTHIESSEN, *The Wind Birds*

EARLY MAY. I force my way through dense brush, following a faint path downhill toward the Browning Passage mudflats. My weather-luck is holding: I'm blessed with another lovely day. Sunlight filters through the forest canopy to illuminate the exuberant vegetation crowding along both sides of the trail. The blue sky is speckled with little clouds drifting out of the northwest.

I have come for a look at one of Clayoquot Sound's most remarkable—and least heralded—natural events. Even before I come to the edge of the forest, I can hear the subjects of my quest, somewhere beyond the screen of trees, talking, singing, quarreling. It's an odd, interesting sound, a faint musical twittering like the distant tinkle of wind chimes—or, as W. H. Hudson wrote: "like the vibrating crystal chiming sounds of a handful of pebbles thrown upon and bounding and glissading musically over a wide sheet of ice."

It's the sound of very many small birds all vocalizing at once.

Over a period of weeks, in late April and early May, whenever the sky clears and the wind comes round to the northwest, great flocks of shorebirds settle onto the mudflats of Tofino Inlet to await the next southeasterly gale. There are whimbrels and godwits. There are dunlins and black-bellied plovers. There are dowitchers and sanderlings and knots. Most especially, there are thousands of tiny western sandpipers keeping company with even tinier least sandpipers. Every single bird is in the midst of its own incredible journey. Already they have come a great distance. Many of them spent the winter—our winter—south of the Equator and most will travel all the way to the high Arctic for a brief breeding season.

This impressive spectacle goes largely unnoticed. When herring gather to spawn, when gray whales arrive on migration, when salmon are running, people sit up and pay attention. But every spring, shorebirds appear by the tens of thousands, spend a few nights and move on without arousing more than a ripple of interest outside a small circle of aficionados.

The general indifference is even more surprising when you consider that this spectacle takes place not in some remote corner of the sound but practically on our doorstep. I didn't even need to get my truck out of the shed this morning. An easy walk, less than half an hour from home, has brought me to this place. Even so, it remains the path less traveled: I have yet to see another human soul.

A LITTLE geography. The village of Tofino lies at the very tip of the Esowista Peninsula, which extends northward from the low country west of Kennedy Lake and includes the Long Beach Unit of Pacific Rim National Park. The peninsula is almost 11 miles (17 kilometers) long, but barely more than a seven hundred feet (two hundred meters) wide in places. Few of the area's visitors, driving the highway back and forth through the green tunnel of forest, realize just how close the ocean presses on both sides.

To the west lies the open Pacific. The outside of the peninsula supports the broad, sandy beaches, surf-swept and restless, for which the area is justly famous: Long Beach, Schooner Cove, Cox Beach, Chesterman Beach, and all the rest.

To the east, Browning Passage cuts between the peninsula and Meares Island. It's a very different sort of environment on that side, much calmer than the open coast, protected from wind and surf, sunnier, warmer. On summer days especially, when the outer coast is shrouded in fog, the warmth radiating from the peninsula's forest is enough to evaporate mist drifting in from the sea. The air over the inlet is clear, the sun bright and hot. The dark expanse of mudflat acts as an enormous solar trap; temperatures can be many degrees higher than on outside beaches. On a rising tide, seawater flowing across the warm mud becomes almost tepid. A good deal of fresh water runoff mixes with the surface layers of seawater.

Wherever significant amounts of sediment-laden fresh water mix with salty, nutrient-rich seawater, a series of chemical and physical interactions cause the suspended material to precipitate in minute particles. Strong tidal currents, sweeping back and forth, keep the main channels of Browning Passage and Tofino Inlet clear. But in sheltered bays where the current is not so strong, particles settle out of the water. Over thousands of years this process has given us a series of enormous mudflats—Arakun Flats, Ducking Flats, Doug Banks Flats, Maltby Slough, South Bay Flats, Grice Bay Flats—mirroring the sandy beaches along the outside of the peninsula.

Mudflats belong to a particularly fascinating category of intertidal ecosystem: the estuary. Estuaries take many forms—mudflats, salt marshes, sloughs, eelgrass meadows—but as a group they comprise some of earth's most productive and useful environments. More sheltered than most intertidal environments and richer in nutrients, estuaries support extraordinary communities of plants and animals.

Central to the economy of these communities is a phenomenon called the detritus cycle. Decomposition of organic material releases minute particles of insoluble residue into the water. Drifting about, these particles of detritus become coated with organic molecules and bacteria.

The coated particles serve as food for filter-feeding animals, clams and such, and for substrate ingestors like
annelid worms. The animals digest what they can and
excrete the insoluble particles to begin the cycle anew. The
detritus-feeders themselves fall prey to predators, which are
taken in turn by larger predators. And so it goes, all the way
up through the trophic pyramid.

Life isn't all a bowl of cherries for estuarine animals and
plants; it's not an easy place to live. Aside from the ever-
present risk of becoming someone else's breakfast, estuarine
organisms must cope with tremendous fluctuations in oxy-
gen levels, salinity, and temperature. Even so, a great many
species depend upon estuaries at some point in their life
cycle. The mudflats of Browning Passage and Tofino Inlet
abound with small fish and invertebrates. The mud is
honeycombed with burrows. It's a fascinating place to
explore, full of bizarre life forms hidden beneath rocks and
buried in the mud. Many of those life forms rate highly on
the shorebird menu. To a flock of sandpipers cruising past
at an altitude of ten thousand feet (three or four thousand
meters), these big mudflats must look well-nigh irresistible.

WHERE MY trail breaks from the forest, I emerge onto a
narrow meadow of grass and sedge along the edge of the
mudflats. The few minutes I spent checking tide charts earlier this morning are proving to be an excellent investment.
The tide is at maximum flood; my timing is perfect. The
inlet is full to the brim and seawater laps gently against the
fringes of shoreline vegetation. The mudflats are completely
submerged, invisible except for a narrow band of brown
ooze along the shore.

Crowded onto that narrow band of mud and vegetation is a packed mass of birds, hundreds and hundreds of individuals, perhaps a dozen different species. The noise is louder here, not unpleasant but steady and insistent. It's a comfortable, conversational sound. The feathered mass shimmers and flickers with constant movement. Birds preen and stretch. Birds quarrel with their neighbors. Birds forage in the mud for food. It's an impressive sight, a vivid mosaic of color and sound.

About three hundred feet (a hundred meters) farther north, the shoreline doubles back into a little bight. A small creek flows from the forest into the sea. The sheltered spit thus formed is one of the best pieces of shorebird habitat in Clayoquot Sound. Moving in that direction, I keep well back from the water, anxious to avoid disturbing the flock.

I needn't have worried. The birds seem to accept my slow-moving presence quite calmly. Perhaps, as far as they're concerned, I'm just a different sort of bear going about my business, which doesn't include eating shorebirds. As it happens, a big black bear comes through here quite regularly; I've met him. These birds probably see that bear every day. I'm just bear number two.

Since I've made my approach in full view, there seems little point in trying to hide now. I pick out a comfortable piece of driftwood and sit down. The birds are so close I hardly need to bother with binoculars. This is wildlife viewing at its most convenient. I watch them; they watch me; everybody's happy. It's an odd setup for bird-watching and I feel almost indecently exposed. But the feathered mass along the shore seems more or less oblivious.

And what a pleasant spot it is. The air is calm. The sun is warm on my shoulders. I've brought a pad along to provide a little insulation from the cold ground, usually most welcome but hardly necessary today.

Browning Passage is at least a mile (a couple of kilometers) wide at this point, a broad panorama. Across the water, the forested slopes of Mount Colnett and Meares Island rise steeply from tidewater. On my left, some distance away, lies the little archipelago of islands at the mouth of Lemmens Inlet that I explored in February. Beyond them, in the distance, the snow-clad peaks of central Vancouver Island— Mount Mariner and all the others—soaring into the blue.

Even from this distance I can see that the deep blue water on the far side of Browning Passage is spangled with whitecaps. A whale-watching boat, returning from a trip to Grice Bay, works its way north along the channel, heading back to Tofino. They're having a rough ride, those folks. The boat is pounding into the chop, throwing up spindrift, clouds of spray. Pretty windy out there, a regular gale out of the northwest. But here, in the sheltered lee of the peninsula, there's barely enough breeze to stir the grass. These birds, seasoned travelers all, know where to stop for a decent meal and good night's rest.

At such close range, the feathered mass resolves itself into individual creatures, even without benefit of magnification. When I train tenpower binoculars on them, the finest details come into focus: legs, beaks, feathers, bright little eyes watching me. *That's better,* I think. That's the way to think of these birds, an important shift in perspective, from flock to individual.

A flock of shorebirds is an extraordinarily tight unit. Anyone who has seen these birds in flight can attest to that. The semaphore flash of wings as hundreds of birds turn in unison, turn and turn, seems almost supernatural. They remind me of the herring schools in Barkley Sound: such perfect coordination. As with the herring, it would be easy to presume that individual birds are little more than automatons programmed by instinct, simple mechanical subunits of a larger machine.

But the close-up view dispels that fallacy. At ease, these birds are as individual as any crowd of tourists: this one is fussing over its toilet, that one is sleeping, yet another is chivvying a neighbor. Doubtless their behavior is shaped largely by instinct—whatever that means—and they do have a strong urge to conform, but shorebirds are not machines. They are conscious of the world around them, processing experience and reacting appropriately, just as human beings do. I have no doubt of their intelligence. Even so, I need to work at taking the next step: not merely thinking of each creature as a self-determined unit governing itself according to the needs of the moment— without, I might add, any benefit of rules, regulations, policies, and procedures—but as an individual with a life and a history.

A couple of weeks ago, that western sandpiper over there, the one stretching its wings, would have been enjoying a tropical beach—in the Caribbean, perhaps, or somewhere along the coast of Peru or Ecuador. It knows what the Pacific coast of North America looks like from sixteen thousand feet (five thousand meters). In a couple of weeks it will have chosen some spot on the tundra in northwest Alaska and be well into the process of creating the next generation of western sandpipers. In short, that little bird leads a more interesting and adventuresome life than I do. Who am I to dismiss it as an automaton, a bundle of reflexes?

Too often, ornithology deals strictly in numbers and occurrences. Birds are treated as little more than vivid objects to be counted, described, tabulated. But each bird is an individual like you and me with its own curriculum vitae: challenges met, successes achieved and calamities suffered. It is interesting to think about what each bird has achieved and what the costs of that achievement might be. The idea of an "average bird" is fiction. Each individual has its own unique life. There are successful birds and there are birds that—for whatever reason, simple bad luck, perhaps— have a difficult time.

Our understanding of shorebirds has grown tremendously in the last fifteen or twenty years. Newer techniques, including radio and satellite telemetry, have revealed amazing things.

These little western sandpipers, for instance, may be flying from Peru to Siberia, muscle power all the way, covering up to 1,100 miles (1,800 kilometers) a day, sometimes staying aloft a day and a half at a time, flying at altitudes up to 3.4 miles (5.5 kilometers). But among shorebirds, they have nothing much to brag about. Sanderlings, not much larger than the westerns, may have come all the way from Tierra del Fuego. Ditto semipalmated plovers. Bristle-thighed curlews migrate from Alaska to Polynesia or New Zealand. Wandering tattlers breed in Alaska and winter as far west as northern New Zealand and the Great Barrier

Reef of Australia. Pacific golden plovers can migrate 2,300 miles (4,500 kilometers) nonstop; those breeding in western Alaska or Siberia may winter as far away as Africa.

. . .

WHEN I pull into Shirley Langer's driveway next morning, the sky is bright overcast. The air is still, but I've a feeling the wind is coming around from northwest to southeast. A change in the weather is on the way. In fact it's just starting to rain: a few scattered drops on the windshield.

Shirley is halfway down the stairs when I reach the house, an older woman, cheerful, binoculars in hand, wearing raincoat and rain pants. She had expressed interest in seeing the birds and we made the arrangements last evening. Adrian Dorst, Tofino's resident ornithologist, will be meeting us at the mudflats.

She laughs as she settles into the passenger seat. "Got your rain gear?"

I nod. "Never leave home without it."

Adrian is just getting out of his van when we arrive. He waves as we pull in. We all walk down to the inlet. It looks very much like yesterday—myriad shorebirds crowded onto the shore by a rising tide—except that today the water is extraordinarily calm. It almost glows, mirroring the brightness of the clouds. We wander along the shore to the spit.

We sit well back from the water at first, enjoying the birds from a distance. Adrian points out the different species for our benefit: western sandpipers, small, with black legs; and least sandpipers, smaller, farther up in the vegetation, with yellow-green legs. A light steady drizzle begins to fall, so gently as to be hardly noticeable, except that our raincoats are soon dripping. The mountains to the north are invisible now, shrouded in cloud and rain.

Adrian wants to get some pictures. He goes down on his belly and squirms forward across the mud. But then he has to back up to get the birds in focus. He's making no attempt at concealment whatever, no blind at all. There are birds all around him, apparently unfazed by this apparition in their midst.

Encouraged by his example, Shirley and I decide that we should get a little bolder too. If he can do it, so can we. Closer to the edge of the water, I lay out my insulated pad for us to share. Then we hunker down, a raincoat bivouac, huddling for warmth.

It's raining steadily now and a breeze from the south ruffles the water. Fortunately it's not cold. It does feel a little odd, sitting calmly in the open, getting rained on. One's natural impulse is to head for cover. (What's the expression? *Too dumb to get out of the rain.*) But it's not uncomfortable once I get used to the idea. In fact, the sight and sound of rain on the water is unexpectedly soothing, almost meditative. It echoes the musical tinkle of the birds talking among themselves. They have calmed down, too. Most are standing quietly, one foot tucked up. Occasionally they rouse to shake the water off their feathers.

I feel increasingly content simply being here, present, not doing anything in particular. In fact, I can't think of a time I've felt more thoroughly engaged with the natural world, part of the whole. The birds seem to think so, too. They had moved away when we took our places, but now they're back. Before long I have western sandpipers foraging within arm's length. A tiny least sandpiper is feeding about an inch (a couple of centimeters) from my right boot. I feel accepted. And so we possess ourselves in patience, waiting for events to come to us.

Eventually the tide begins to draw away. The birds grow restless. Soon it will be time for them to move back onto the newly exposed flats and continue feeding. And the southeast wind is rising, rising.

Suddenly it's over. The moment is past. The flocks are taking wing. Shirley's knees have had enough and I'm aware of the water trickling down my back. I suddenly remember that there are places I have to be, chores that need doing.

Over the water, a great flock of western sandpipers whirls back and forth, like smoke in the wind. The weaving mass flashes white one moment, dark the next, as the birds show first the undersides of their wings, then the upper surfaces, all in perfect unison. Higher and higher they dance, up and down, around and around, finally over the trees and out of sight, lost in the mist.

WESTERN SANDPIPERS belong to a cluster of species, small shorebirds familiarly known to birders as "peeps." Typically found in large mixed flocks, peeps forage across mudflats and sandy beaches, sometimes venturing up into the shore-line vegetation, picking and probing for food with a busy sewing-machine motion. They are all tiny birds, sparrow-sized except for their long narrow wings. Western sandpipers, for example, tip the scales at a scanty ounce (28 grams) (a golf ball weighs about 1.6 ounces [45 grams]).

In winter, western sandpipers occupy an enormous range of coastline on both the Pacific (from British Columbia to Peru) and the Atlantic (from New England to Brazil).

In contrast, their summer breeding range is surprisingly restricted: northwest Alaska and the Chukotskiy Peninsula in extreme eastern Siberia.

Perhaps the species was a casualty of rising sea levels at the end of the last ice age. Alaska and the Chukotskiy would have been part of the same land mass during the Pleistocene. Little groups of human nomads making their way across the Bering land bridge during those brief Arctic summers must have flushed great flocks of breeding western sandpipers. Then came warmer temperatures, melting glaciers and the ever-encroaching ocean. Perhaps migrating western sand-pipers, even now, are chasing some dim ancestral memory of a great, rich, sea-level plain, long gone beneath the waves—a sort of avian Atlantis.

In springtime, when the world's entire population of western sandpipers gathers into one narrow corridor for the migration north, they become the most numerous shore-bird on the Pacific coast of North America. Major estuaries host from a quarter to one million individuals at a time. The birds move from estuary to estuary in stepping-stone fash-ion: San Francisco and Humboldt bays; Bolinas Lagoon; Gray's Harbor; the Fraser, Stikine, Fox, and Copper river deltas; Cook Inlet; Redoubt and Kachemak bays. The males pass through first, hurrying northward to stake out territory. Females follow.

Westerns nest on well-drained tundra from sea-level plains to low mountain slopes. They prefer mixed habitat: ridges and hummocks of heath, with wetlands—marshes, pools, and lakes—close at hand. Suitable country can sup-port a high population, with each pair defending a tiny territory, cheek by jowl with their neighbors. They feed mostly on insects, foraging both wet and dry heath. Western sandpipers are monogamous. The female lays four eggs, usually hidden under bushy cover. Both sexes share incubation duties, beginning when the last egg is laid. Twenty-one days later, the eggs hatch.

The chicks are extremely precocious, able to move about and start foraging for themselves almost immediately. Mom abandons the family shortly afterwards. Dad chaperones the kids until they fledge, just nineteen days after hatching; then he takes off too. (Which makes for an interesting reversal of human norms: not only does Mom leave Dad to care for the kids, but when the kids grow up, their parents leave home.) From then on, the young of the year must fend for themselves. They migrate on their own.

Let me repeat that, in case you missed it. The youngsters, barely a month old, make that first migration entirely on their own. The first southbound adults turn up on the beaches of western Vancouver Island in late June. Adult migration peaks in mid-July then falls off rapidly. The first juveniles show up in late July; how they manage is anybody's guess. Research suggests that bonds forged during first migration may last a lifetime, with little flocks from a given year-class feeding together, migrating together, perhaps breeding together.

Most southward-migrating western sandpipers follow a trans-Pacific route that carries them out across the Gulf of Alaska to a landfall somewhere in southern British Columbia or the northwestern United States. That means thousands of miles across open water at altitudes up to three miles (five and a half kilometers). Pretty much the whole population funnels through the Pacific northwest before dispersing to wintering areas on both sides of the continent.

Now, here's the really interesting bit.

A group of ornithologists around Rob Butler at the Canadian Wildlife Service gathered and analyzed data on weight loss and gain during migration. They considered the length of stay at various rest stops. They calculated the energy costs, hence expected weight loss, for various legs of the journey. And they discovered—even assuming maximum stopovers at estuaries, maximum rates of fat deposition and minimum energy expenditure during flight—that the birds could not possibly cover that vast distance in calm conditions and maintain their body weight. I'll put that another way. Flying in calm conditions, absolutely still air, birds that started the trip in tip-top shape should theoretically lose weight steadily en route and arrive on the breeding grounds fatally emaciated, literally skin and bones. All those birds that can be seen arriving on breeding territory in fine shape would need to deposit fat at impossible rates—0.1 ounces (three grams) a day or more, compared to observed rates of 0.01 to 0.03 ounces (one-third to one gram) a day—to make the trip in calm conditions.

It was a mystery.

The sandpipers couldn't possibly be taking on enough calories to cover the rigors of the trip. How were they managing? Well, as any manager knows, when revenue isn't sufficient to sustain the enterprise, the only alternative is to cut costs and improve efficiency. Westerns reduce drag by flying in flock formation—birds in flocks may gain up to three miles (five kilometers) an hour over birds flying alone.

Sandpipers also get more free speed by traveling at high altitudes—flight speeds increase five percent for each additional three thousand feet (thousand meters) of altitude.

Most significantly, they harness the winds, exploiting the favorable, avoiding the unfavorable. Air masses circulating counterclockwise around low-pressure systems in the Gulf of Alaska are the key to their strategy. In spring, birds can ride southeasterly winds along the eastern edge of a convenient low, up the Pacific coast and into Alaska. After breeding, they hop aboard the same circulation, this time riding it down the west side of the low, going far out over the Pacific and then back toward the west coast of British Columbia. They may even be skilled, like hot-air balloonists, at exploring different altitudes to find the most favorable wind. Truly they are "wind birds." The distances are so immense that they dare not battle a headwind: they don't have sufficient metabolic fuel. When conditions are favorable, they can stay aloft for days at a time, covering thousands of miles at a stretch. But if the wind blows contrary, they must get out of the sky and find someplace suitable to rest, stoke up, and await the next ride.

The birds are absolutely dependent on those fueling stations. With their energy budgets so carefully calculated— migration on a shoestring—they cannot afford to lose any sources of revenue. They also need places to come ashore after that long ride over the Pacific, quiet places where they're not going to get chased up and down the beach by someone's dog.

So conserving shorebirds means conserving estuaries. There are, unfortunately, precious few large estuaries on the Pacific coast of North America. And like most forms of wetland, estuaries are being lost to development at a fierce rate, especially in urban areas but also in relatively pristine places like Clayoquot Sound. Even here, development encroaches year by year: more houses, more people, more pets. It's ironic that just when the loss of habitat elsewhere is making the Tofino mudflats more and more important, they themselves should come under pressure.

· · ·

THE FRONT has passed during the night. A pale sun shows through flying cloud-wisps. Along the path, bushes are dripping and puddles have collected in the hollows among the roots. All is quiet, except for the songs of woodland birds.

Again, the tide is perfect, high and full. Water laps calmly on the shore. But nobody's here. The inlet seems vacant, empty, almost desolate.

I walk toward the spit. Nothing rises from the water's edge or from the grass. The rain has erased all tracks from the mud. Except for the odd feather or bit of down clinging to the wrack along the high-tide line, there is no trace of the great flocks. They might almost have been, beginning and end, an illusion.

At the tip of the spit, I put up one solitary bird, a dowitcher. Perhaps there's something wrong with it; couldn't keep up and so was left behind. It flies off, calling, alone and forlorn.

I sit down and scan the inlet with binoculars. Far out across the water toward Browning Passage and Meares Island, a small flock of something semaphores its presence with a brief flash of white. The flock turns and vanishes into its surroundings. Otherwise the place is deserted.

I wait and watch until the tide starts to withdraw. The sun picks up strength. The air is warm. But nothing comes in. The birds are gone.

It's another instance of nature's flywheel moving relentlessly forward. Yesterday's flocks will be far to the north now. Some of the birds that were here two days ago may already have reached the Stikine River delta in Alaska. This is life in the fast lane. Shorebirds have long migrations and short breeding seasons. By mid-summer, less than two months from now, they'll be stopping here again, *on their way back south*. They haven't a moment to lose.

I understand that, but I miss them all the same. The sun is shining; there is promise of a beautiful day ahead. But life seems to have left this place. The excitement has gone elsewhere, following those birds. I imagine the flocks flying northward over a wild landscape of rugged mountains, dark forest, deep fjords. They are heading toward the danger and promise of an Arctic summer. I wish I could go. It's a bad case of *zugunruhe,* migration restlessness, cabin fever. I feel it every springtime and every autumn too.

Perhaps that's why shorebirds have such strong resonance, even for people with no particular interest in birds. They appeal to the nomad in all of us. They awaken some restless vestige of an earlier time—not all that long ago, in the great scheme of things—when human beings had not yet abandoned migration.

RITUAL

. . . .

(JOHN HAY)

THE MONTH of May streams forward, in all its sequences of light. The air warms up, while southerly winds still battle with the north. In this transmigratory period, it still seems miraculous to me not that these seabirds can find their way, but that they possess such a sureness of place, from one pole to the other. It is a magic of fitness, of appropriate measure on a global scale, which they carry in their minds.

In terms of their behavior, terns are so spontaneous as to be inseparable from the present. At the same time, they exist in an eternal present insofar as they follow the dictates of the sun and the earth's travels around it. In a highly seasonal part of the world, we divide the year into spring, summer, autumn, and winter, but ultimately only one season dictates the infinitely varied terms of life to all creation.

The clouds are only temporarily described by our classifica-
tion of them into cirrus, nimbus, stratus cumulus, and their
variations. They take their forms from continuous motion,
and those beings who follow that motion in themselves
can never be on a lower scale than ourselves, who see fit
to determine all stages of it in terms of material possession
and the human mind. As played out in the birds, the plan-
etary rhythms have a supremacy which cannot be violated
or reduced. The terns arrive on their territories, as they will
leave them, obeying certain time-honored rituals, which
amount to a high form of courtesy which we might do well
to respect.

The terns are in a state of great urgency as they gather
offshore and begin to move in, aggravated in their need to
pair up and nest. In the vicinity of the nesting site at Gray's
Beach, a female is making constant, chittering cries as she
waits on a sandbar for attention. A male hovers over a tide-
pool nearby, then twists in the air and makes a slanting dive
into the surface to pick up a minnow, which he brings to her.
The fish is accepted and swallowed, but she goes on begging,
and he tries it twice again while I watch, to finally break off
and leave her there, perhaps to be more satisfied by him, or
another possible mate, later on. These early indecisions are
common enough in courtship, but they might contain some
underlying doubt as to whether or not the birds have come
to the right place.

Gulls circle and romp together in the springtime air,
while others are scattered over the tidal flats, musically calling. A man and his girlfriend go idling and bumping each
other down the beach, swaying like trees in a wind. I walk
out over the complex map of the tidelands, across their

ripples and watery lanes and shallow pools. It is a silvery landscape and the sky is sending down light showers like so much sea spray.

Water spurts up from a hole made by a clam. As the tide begins to move in, wavelets bob and duck around me, gradually covering and wreathing the sands. Through my field glasses, I see a pair of common terns strutting around each other, heads and necks stretched up, tails cocked, wings lowered and held out partly on their sides.

Further out over the sands is a pair of roseate terns, recognizable through their black bills, their longer tails, and feathers of a more uniformly light gray than the commons. They get their name from a pinkish flush on their breasts, not always visible except when the light strikes them at the right angle. The stance of these birds when courting is extremely elegant. Their tails project behind them like spars on a sailing vessel. Their velvety gray wings spread out like a cloak, the hem nearly touching the ground, and their shining black heads and beaks point cleanly toward the sky, in a pose that is highly strict and formalized.

On both sides of the Atlantic, the population of roseates has seriously declined. In America, they have been classified as an endangered species. The common terns, more aggressive and adaptable, have managed to hold their own for the time being, but not without help from individuals and institutions protecting their nesting site. Roseates are more vulnerable to the twentieth century's worldwide disturbances, and are disappearing . . . a bird of classic style that ought to be as precious to us as the Parthenon has been to the Greeks. But we let the great architecture of life slip away from us and what we no longer see before us we are unable, or unwilling, to compare with the lesser standards by which we value the earth.

Many of the birds engaging in courtship behavior before they settle in to nest have been premated, which is to say, paired up during the previous season. Either they have spent the winter together, or they have recognized each other on arriving in the vicinity of the site. Even though premated pairs will start in to court and nest without much delay, just as many seem to join the majority in days of ground and aerial display. This is a process through which pairs are finally "bonded," and the whole colony established. It is difficult at first to tell the difference between males and females, until pairs start to copulate before nesting. In these early days, three, four, or five birds displaying together is quite common, which makes distinguishing between the sexes even harder.

(I do not know of any ready shortcut to identifying males and females. Years ago, the warden of a colony of Sandwich and common terns in Great Britain told me that he could tell the difference by their voices. Since he had been listening to them all his life, as had his father before him, I had no reason to doubt him. He also contended that he could tell male from female by the way the black cap ended at the nape of the neck; it comes to more of a point in the male, and is a little squared off or blunted in the female. So far, at least, this last distinction has not worked for me, since the shape of the black feathers on their necks seems to depend on the way they happen to be holding their heads, up or down.)

J.M. Cullen, in her thesis on the Arctic terns, describes an action she calls tilting in the mating display of the Arctics; the behavior of the commons is almost identical. These and other species have fully developed black caps during the breeding season, but their fall molt leaves them with a streaked or grayish patch on their heads, and a whitish forehead. The conclusion is that the black cap has a definite function during mating. In displaying before a potential mate, a bird will tilt its head so that the cap is hidden, or partly turned away from its partner. To show it directly seems to have an intimidating effect. If a female walks around a male in a "bent" position, with her beak pointed toward the ground—as opposed to an "erect" display with head and neck pointed upward—the male on his inside circle makes an effort to keep his cap turned away from her, because if she catches sight of it, she might move away.

Since males are probably made nervous, or put off, by the display of the cap as well, and since they are more aggressive than females in defense of territory, the display may have some significance as a threat, but is probably used more in avoidance and appeasement than as a direct challenge. If a male pecks at a female, or rushes toward her, she will tilt her cap to avoid further trouble, and males startled or frightened by something during a mating display, or while making their way through a neighbor's territory, will do the same.

Step by step, from the first hesitant approaches to the territory, to early nesting behavior, followed by established nests, egg laying, and the raising of chicks, the season is followed out with formality and underlying discipline. After the terns have begun to settle in, the sands are covered with little chain patterns made by their feet where they have strutted around each other, while a high and wide chasing, fluttering up, circling, and gliding goes on overhead, at times loose, easy, and pliable, and at others very fast. All this effort leads up to a means whereby a colony can occupy old nests, or establish new ones over a given space, with order and understood boundaries. (On some islands, pairs of terns have been seen coming back to their exact same nesting sites over a period of many years.) In general, a male attempts to lead a female down to a proposed site, often with several males chasing after him, especially if he is carrying a fish. The sorting out takes days on end; it amounts to a continual trying out, a continual falling short, or erosion, of the efforts of males and females to form their "pair bonds."

Males may even put a great deal of effort into trying to attract birds that may not be the right sex in the first place, such as a male who seems to be behaving momentarily like a female, or a female that is already mated. Sex recognition often takes time. The combination of attack and escape that is part of all their efforts to mate is also a factor in temporarily holding them back from the serious business of nesting. They are edgy. They engage in maneuvers which are broken off, time and again. But sooner or later, a female becomes satisfied that her suitor has chosen the right space of chosen ground to nest in.

(Much of the time spent in finding an appropriate mate probably has an element of critical judgment in it, so far as the female is concerned. She needs a mate who is going to bring in plenty of fish and choose a good nesting hollow in the first place, and that implies discrimination.)

Scraping out little hollows in the sand represents an early stage in courtship ritual, but it is a practice that serves to strengthen emotional ties. (Emotion plays a very strong part in the life of these birds.) After a male and female greet each other, posturing, the male may walk over to a preexisting hollow which he has chosen, then lower his breast while scratching out backward in the sand. If the female is interested enough, she may go over and stand by him, or even replace her suitor to enlarge the scrape on her own. Such scrapes are often called false by the ornithologists because they do not lead to a final nest.

In a similar way, the presentation of fish on the ground is another ceremonial act that strengthens their feelings toward each other. A male parading with a fish before a prospective mate does a sort of goose step, breast forward, in a very conscious way. It is an athlete or a soldier strutting his stuff, displaying his medals or his victorious presence before the girls. She begs for this precious gift, bent down in a submissive posture, while making eager, chittering cries like a chick being fed by its parent. At times she takes the fish, swallows it, and then flies away without any obvious sign of gratitude. Or a tension between them results in a tug-of-war. She snatches at the fish, and he holds on so that they are left with two halves.

In another version of this behavior, the female grabs at the fish and the male flies away with it, as if displeased. They share contradictory feelings at this stage of the game. She has a compulsion to lay eggs, and he to start in on the nest. This results in slight acts of aggression. The inner testing that marks their attempts to pair up implies that the male may be just as frightened as the female, or enough afraid of her so as not to surrender the fish.

As I watch them, distant as they are from my own sense of reality, I sense something of my own ambivalence. Seasons of hesitation, nerves sprung in the wind, characterize us both. On a deeper level, all this avian maneuvering with its wayward rhythms follows an uncompromising need that brings energy into our own affairs and fear to our hearts.

As the days go by, the activity becomes more intense. At least a few terns are displaying whenever I walk out over the marsh to watch them, at a viewing distance. One of a pair might be on the ground with wings cloaked and tail cocked, while the other circles over it. Three will land simultaneously. With necks craned in the same direction and wings held out, they look like uniformed soldiers on dress parade. Swift chases are going on in the air, involving three, or as many as five or six at a time. They are constantly engaged in flying up from the sandy hollows and hummocks, leading away, breaking off, settling down again, and day by day, the general clamor increases.

In their wild, formal, and repeated exercises, they also interchange with the sandy land they came to. Their rituals are rhythmically allied with the growing grasses now shaking and whipping in the wind, and with the waters trickling back and forth over the tidal flats, shivering, parting, coming together again under silken clouds.

Courtship flights follow the two main types of ground display, combining elements of both. A male with beak pointed downward, as in the bent display, tries to lead a female who adopts the erect posture, or a less extreme equivalent of it, with head and neck extended and tilted upward. They fly past each other, each one alternately falling behind and overtaking the other so that it looks as if they were swinging in the air.

When a male carries a fish on these flights, as a superior form of attraction, it often starts with three or more birds engaging in much evasive action, eventually evolving into two. The remaining pair then fly off together, interchanging positions as they go. The bird in front may swing downward and to the side, while the other flies over and past it. Then the procedure is reversed as the bird now in the lead moves back and downward. There is a lovely, tilting balance to their flight. The male makes a clear *keera,* while the female may cry *kip-kip* or *tik-tik,* and then his call may change to a rasping *koh-koh-keearrh.*

So the sorting out in the colony goes on and on, and I hear many other cries as the birds go through their nearly incessant flying up and landing again, many stridently challenging, connective cries. Isn't this urgent practice, for days on end, what we are continually required to do, at times veering off wildly in the wrong direction?

The tension in these flights, the resolution of conflict in these rituals, is in the spring itself, where the ruffed grouse drums and the gulls bow to each other. No life lacks ceremony.

The tension of opposites lies behind the perfection of form and all appearances. So a leaf stirs in the wind and lifts like a bird; the insect is the image of the leaf it inhabits; the shiny seed of a red maple has a cracked back like a winged beetle. Unlikeness seeks out likeness everywhere. Throughout these relationships, unendingly renewed, are the elements of evasion and affinity, touch and recoil. The hunger generated in the worlds of life, the fish to rise and be met by a predatory bird, the fish to suspend or procreate in the tension of the waters, is back of all memory and behavior.

The more I see of courtship fights, the more they compare with human games. The natural ease of all great ball players is in them, of champion skaters, or ballet dancers. At the same time, I doubt whether there is much that can equal their high flight and its glide to earth. This culminating flight involves the circling upward of a pair to a high altitude, with one bird leading the other. At some point, one of them folds its wings slightly and starts to glide easily toward the ground, while the other follows. The two of them bank back and forth from one side to the other, swaying and side-slipping together as if their whole life had been a training for such an act.

The roseates, a cut in elegance above the commons, have a beautifully reaching look to their bodies as they glide together. When a pair flies slowly over the territory, their wings, stroking with an effortless assurance that accompanies the steady flow of a wave, appear to lean and hang on the air. Pairs of both species will circle high over a colony, but the roseates often fly out in a great circling fetch over the sea. I have watched a pair of roseates rising so high in the brilliantly blue sky that I have almost lost sight of them, but their impeccable snowy feathers shone in the light of the sun, while their catamaran-like tails showed as white filaments. (Their tails are longer and more flexible than the commons, floating and bouncing on the wind.) Their skill is dazzling. In a strong wind, they look as if they were flying backward as they ascend, but they are in perfect control. With both commons and roseates, a very fast chasing and circling upward will often end in a wide zigzagging glide down.

Roseates arrive on the nesting grounds later than the commons, although their spring migration is probably faster, since they are superior flyers. While common terns move up the coastline, relatively close to the shore, roseates fly higher and farther out over the ocean. By early to mid-June, after most of the commons are incubating eggs, or brooding chicks, some roseates will still be engaged in courtship flights. Nothing exceeds their slip-streaming across the sky, incomparably lithe and limber. At times they skate through the sky as if shot from a sling, and at others they sail like kites on a high wind, or knife through the air like mackerel in undulant waters. They remind me then of William Blake's "arrows of desire."

Both species make spectacular glides. After a passage of synchronized swinging, they appear to start tumbling, or revolving high in the air. This is apparently due to a form of gliding in which they turn as they fall, tilting one wing over the other in a vertical instead of horizontal plane. Whereas common terns may start a downward glide from five or six hundred feet (150 or 180 meters), and Roseates from still higher, Sandwich Terns will circle up to several thousand feet. I have been told that from that great height, a pair will drop at a speed of sixty to seventy miles (ninety-five to 110 kilometers) an hour, the pressure on their outer primary feathers making a papery, drumming sound. They plunge down toward the ternery at an angle of about sixty degrees until they are within three to four hundred feet (ninety to 120 meters) of the ground, then sheer upward, to circle and land in an easy, finished way together. The whole arc of this masterful performance may take in as much as two miles (just over three kilometers). What a surpassing way to express the feelings of opposite sexes freed of their restraint!

A friend of mine once said to me as I was rhapsodizing about this dance of the birds: "How does that relate to me? Tell us about *ourselves.*" Hadn't I suggested parallels enough?

I realize that very few of us, even when we are in love, have the ability to launch into paired maneuvers a thousand feet in the air. But I suspect that what stopped him from making the connection was the idea of "nature," which he had long since left to the scientists and sentimentalists.

Courtship in animals follows certain stereotyped patterns that go back so far in the vast flow of evolution that we can only guess as to their origins. In that sense alone there is no use oversimplifying these rituals in our favor. Accustomed to pigeons billing and cooing in the city, people are inclined to think of birds as helplessly repetitive, incapable of reflecting on their own actions. Year after year, I have heard it said of the alewives, they just come back and do the same thing. Yet these fish, on their annual journey, are once again engaged in a revolutionary mission. To put down the birds in their sexual flights and courtship rituals is to underrate the profundity of the rhythm of the year. It also passes over their closeness to earth environments whose every mood may be a matter of life and death.

In the existence of a tern, love as we know it may be only an incident, which if at all relevant, seems to be a high degree made up of aggravation. Yet in a short season, they carry out the paramount needs of love, and we ought not to be so niggardly or self-limiting as to deny it to them. The same, imperative inner demands send us ahead on our own migrations. Subconscious motivation is a common property of life. We are unable to escape our origins.

The inner conflict between nesting pairs and its resolution comes out of an earth engagement as mysterious as anything we will ever know. The term "pair bond" seems excessively limited by comparison.

Wild chases, accompanied by a great deal of clamor, increase as more birds come in and the colony establishes itself. The friction between attraction and intimidation fires their energies. At times, the elements of hostility which is a part of their flights gives way to a fight, usually short-lived. A pair may start off easily enough but then drop to the ground with angry, gargling cries, in a flurry of beating wings. Or two birds, wings rapidly stroking, will rise from the territory, partly turning around each other and moving backward at the same time. The one rises above the other, and they will keep alternating in this way, each trying to be the one on top. It is an action that has some of the characteristics of a fight between two males on the ground, but often turns into a paired flight that looks like courtship. These "flutter-ups" are mainly associated with nesting territory, and play some part in the recognition by individual birds of their separate claims—which leads to the idea that they are engaged in by males.

A vigorous fight starts up between two male roseates on the ground. They peck violently at each other, wings beating, but quickly break off. It might be said that the fight has served to define a mutual tolerance, an understanding that can be translated into a few inches of territory.

Roseates, as compared with the commons, which like more open ground, choose fairly thick vegetation to nest in, often making small, tunnellike openings at the edge of a heavy growth of grass. In some areas, they also nest under boulders or in rock burrows where they are narrowly confined, and where mating rituals have to be performed in a highly stylized manner. The male goes in first, followed by the female. She starts by facing him, then pivots around, posturing, while he lowers his head, calling *uh-uh-uh-uh*. Then the female goes back out, while he engages in some scraping motions. Terns know where their boundaries are, though they may be invisible to us, especially out in the open, but rock walls enforce proximity, and the ritual has to be precisely carried out, or the pair will fight.

On open ground, a pair of roseates weave around each other in tight little circles, like matadors with their capes, while bowing and craning their glossy black heads, tail feathers held up behind their silvery backs, wings bowed out at their sides. There is something stiff and military about it. This is a ritual which is perfectly tuned to the rhythms of space and cannot be transgressed. Its formality does not allow the slightest deviation, being no more tyrannical, no less pure than those ice crystals I see forming on the water's surface as winter comes. We invent our instruments, each one an improvement on the last in our efforts to surpass the bonds of nature, but life's perfected instruments are bound to laws beyond our ability to see.

A male common tern flies in with a fish and offers it to his prospective mate, having tried it before without success. At last, the right signal has been received. She takes the fish and eats it, and he is stimulated to copulate with her. He circles her, four or five times over, while she turns, only slightly, after which he mounts her, standing high on her back of a minute, then quickly lowering to copulate. Then he postures briefly and they both fly off.

During the action another bird stands nearby, posturing in a sort of half-hearted way, as if it entertained the notion of joining them. For terns, three is not always a crowd. I have heard of a case in which an unmated male joined a pair that was already engaged in incubating eggs and was allowed to help. It sounds as if the married couple just got accustomed to having him around and gave him a key to the home, but there is a less whimsical explanation for it. Among various kinds of breeding birds there are unmated individuals, not sexually engaged with the nesting parents, who may help with incubating eggs, or even with the feeding and rearing of the young. Such helpers are often younger birds who are in a sense shut out. They have difficulty in colonies where space is zealously guarded and occupied. As independents, they are not able to find a place to breed or obtain a mate.

Efforts at copulation do not always succeed right away. A male may mount a female and stand on her back for minutes at a time, teetering a little in an absent-minded way before he climbs off, with nothing accomplished. Repeated efforts are often made, but with consummation, egg laying soon follows.

In another part of the colony, a bird slightly enlarges a scrape in the sand, digging out backward while his mate stands aside. Then he stands back while she moves in to the nest, plucking lightly at some grass. Finally both posture, circling each other, and then stand together on the nest facing into the wind, with an air of proud attachment.

THE VALLEY *of the* CRANE

· · · ·

(JIM MILLER)

· I ·

...and so grey-eyed Athene swept through the host of
the Achaians, urging them forward into battle...and
they were like the multitudinous nations of birds wing-
ing, of geese, and of cranes, and of swans long-throated
in the Asian meadows beside the Kaystrian waters, as
this way and that they make their flights in the pride
of their wings, then settle in clashing swarms and the
whole meadow echoes with them, so did the Greeks
from their ships and shelters pour forth unto the plain
of Skamandros, thousands of them...

HOMER, *The Iliad,* Book II

As I stepped from the cottonwoods under the last March stars I expected to see cranes, large numbers of cranes. Instead, I saw only the river—black water in the gray pre-dawn. A chilly breeze was blowing and I raised the collar of my jacket as I approached the ruined wooden bridge. The single narrow lane had not seen any traffic in a long time, but the bridge afforded a good view of the country in all directions. Here the river was maybe half a mile (nearly one kilometer) wide and divided by several sandbars, the largest of which separated the channel into two parts, and these islands were mostly overgrown with willows and sedges. On either bank the cottonwoods and alders grew thickly in the deep soil of the flood plain. Once these sandy bottomlands knew the moccasins of dancing Pawnee villagers and visiting French *coureur du bois,* the splayed paws of prairie wolves and the autumnal thunder of bison hooves. Now, the valley of the Platte was dedicated largely to agriculture, and otherwise supported only a few reclusive deer and curious opossums, the occasional raccoon or coyote.

For some reason the area around the bridge must have been unattractive to the cranes; perhaps it had served as a vantage point for hunters in the days when cranes were still a game species in Nebraska. Or perhaps some fool had harassed the birds in more recent times—I'd heard about people driving their cars in darkness to the water's edge and then hitting the headlights in order to give their children a close-up view of the roosting cranes. Whatever the reason, I couldn't see a single bird, although the swelling cacophony downstream left little doubt as to their whereabouts—just out of sight, but certainly not trying to hide.

Despite being forewarned, I was unprepared for the sheer volume of their calls, and it was getting louder by the minute. My overall impression was of a riotous free-for-all, out of control, about to explode. It was a din unlike any that I had ever heard, a haunting, otherworldly sound. And it was the sound that had already been heard for ages when this river, the Platte River, was born.

For 60 million years, the call of the sandhill crane has echoed across the world's wetlands and waterways, and it's been heard in North America for at least 9 million years. Sandhill cranes, the oldest living bird species, have seen the violent birthing of entire mountain ranges, and then watched these same massifs experience slow death at the hands of wind and rain. These enduring birds have witnessed the ebb and flow of vast seas of water and ice. Long before man first took feeble steps on two legs, or raised a rock in anger, sandhills were already ancient. Many species that were once contemporaries of sandhill cranes now survive only as fossils in museum collections or as hatch marks on geologic timelines. Today, cranes occur on every continent except South America, but of the fourteen extant species, most are rare, including the only other North American species, the highly endangered whooping crane. Still, sandhills survive in great numbers. And each spring 80 percent of the world's population, half a million strong, descend on an eighty-mile (129-kilometer) stretch of the Platte River in south-central Nebraska.

The sun had not yet broken the horizon when the first cranes began to rise from their riverine night roost. A few isolated groups ascended at first and then gradually they increased in frequency, taking off to the southeast and into the wind. While an entire roosting flock numbers in the thousands, I estimated most of these groups to be about fifty or sixty birds. Once airborne, the flocks scattered to all points of the compass. One after another, in an endless procession they rose. Some flocks wheeling and turning in such a tight circle that the lead birds were flying in the opposite direction from the cranes bringing up the rear, their wings nearly touching. Occasionally there would be a lull in take-off activity accompanied by a decrease in the volume of calls, and I thought that perhaps I had seen the last. But soon the general clamor would again rise in volume and yet another bunch would take to the wing.

The formations appeared quite fluid with individuals shifting and trading positions—heads thrust forward, necks straight, and legs trailing. Some angled overhead, flying low but never directly upriver, and I could see individual birds in dusky gray plumage and hear distinct voices clearly as they passed. The typical call was a ratchety three-note trill. My friend Howard, who's read everything on cranes from the popular literature to the ornithological journals, but insists that he's learned the most by just watching, told me that the birds mate for life and that through their incessant calling are able to keep track of one another in all the commotion, at least that's the idea.

Indeed, crane music plays an important role in mediating many social interactions. Calls are used to advertise territories and to co-ordinate take-offs and landings, in pair bonding and pair maintenance, to signal the presence of a potential threat, and to synchronously bring pair members into sexual readiness. The sandhill crane is uniformly equipped to produce calls with subtle harmonic nuances. The trachea, or windpipe, of a typical adult is about forty-eight inches (122 centimeters) long, more than twice the length of its neck, and this remarkable piece of sandhill anatomy allows the bird to produce a rich variety of vocalizations at a fairly high volume.

Now and then I'd see a lone crane flying back and forth, apparently seeking a familiar answer to its forlorn cries. According to Howard, when mates become separated or if a juvenile loses its parent, the birds will search in earnest until the family is reunited. My heart went out to these loners—I felt as though I'd been through this sort of thing myself a time or two.

The sun was up now and activity began to wane. I made my way back through the cottonwoods, periodically looking up to catch a glimpse of a few passing stragglers.

· II ·

The Platte, called by the Otoes Ne-Braska, (Flat river, or water) is, as its name imports, almost uniformly broad and shoal. It is fordable at almost any place, except when swollen by freshets, which occur in the Spring season, from melting of snow . . . its bed is composed almost exclusively of sand, forming innumerable bars . . . Large herds of bison were in every direction . . . blackening the whole surface of the country through which we passed.

EDWIN JAMES, botanist and geologist for the 1820
expedition of Major Stephen H. Long

"Check it out!"

It was mid-afternoon and I had connected with Howard. He was pointing to a long, undulating flock, circling just above the tall grass about half a mile out (eight hundred meters). Not cranes this time. Howard stopped the pickup and poked his 10×50 Redfields out of the driver's side. He was a big, red-bearded man, maybe six-foot-five (1.95 meters), and any repositioning in the cramped cab was an effort attended by a certain amount of grunting and groaning.

"White-fronted geese."

We'd been driving for several hours through an area called the Rainwater Basin, which covers 4,200 square miles (10,800 square kilometers) in central Nebraska just south of the Platte River. It's a mosaic of private agricultural land, used extensively for dryland farming and deep well irrigation as well as grasslands, wetlands, a wildlife refuge, and forty-five WPAS (waterfowl production areas). Administered by the U.S. Fish and Wildlife Service, these scattered parcels consist of wet meadows and uncultivated fields, some flooded to form expansive, shallow lakes that serve as critical staging areas for between 7 million and 9 million geese, ducks, and shorebirds on their way north during spring migration. Howard was giving me the grand tour.

It was a little past three when we turned north into one of these WPAS and began zigzagging our way slowly across a grid of gravel roads. Just as we passed a cottonwood that was showing the first green buds of the year, I glimpsed a Swainson's hawk quick-diving into an irrigation ditch adjacent to the road, out of sight. We'd been seeing quite a few raptors all day—mainly Swainson's and harriers, but more than a few redtails and several eagles, both golden and bald.

"Good Lord."

Howard stopped the truck on a one-lane causeway, flooded meadows on either side. On the left, coots bobbed close to the road. But about halfway out, the lake on the right turned white from shore to shore.

"Snow geese. There must be 20,000 of them."

I stepped out of the cab and into ankle-deep mud. Another couple of feet and it would have been knee-deep water. Howard was right, this avian carpet was about 80 percent snow geese, but through the binoculars I could see that at least half a dozen other waterfowl species were also represented. We stood and stared for about fifteen minutes, when I noticed a Chevy sedan sitting behind us. The couple inside were waiting patiently. Waiting was their only option unless they wanted to drive about a quarter-mile (four hundred meters) in reverse. We moved on.

Howard and I first met in Boulder, Colorado, in the early 1980s and became fast friends. I was a house painter at the time, and Howard was a finish carpenter and custom furniture maker. One of the best. He moved back to his native Nebraska in 1985 and married a local girl, Drew. Two wise and well-considered choices. He wasn't bringing down the same kind of money that he'd been accustomed to in upscale Boulder, but that was okay. He'd inherited a little cottage and a piece of bottomland on the Platte. An intelligent and down-to-earth wife (and damned pretty), low overhead, working at a craft he enjoys, plenty of free time—all in all, success. With the river pretty much in his backyard, he'd taken quite an interest in the Platte ("the

great lost river" as he calls it), and especially in the cranes,
the same cranes that he largely took for granted as a kid.

As we bounced along, I thought of the bridge and turned
to Howard.

"Why the Platte?"

Howard smiled.

"Why the great lost river? Picture an hourglass. These
birds come in from Texas, New Mexico, the Gulf coast,
ultimately bound for their breeding grounds on the northern plains or on the Arctic coast from Canada to Siberia,
depending on which subspecies we're talking about. Three
subspecies of sandhills share the Platte River Valley. Mostly
the lesser, but also the Canadian and the greater sandhill. They come together to rest and build up fat reserves,
maybe 10 percent of their body weight in a month, for the
trip north and for breeding. It's a long trip, maybe 6,000
miles (10,000 kilometers). They need two things—a reliable source of food and a safe place to roost between meals."

I could tell that Howard, like a practiced university hall
lecturer, had given this spiel a time or two, and that, unlike
most of the lecturers that I'd been exposed to, he enjoyed
giving it.

"They used to rely on the marshes and wet meadows
along the river, but those are mostly gone now—no money
in wetlands. But the fact that cranes are opportunists has
allowed them to continue making a living around here. It's
kind of ironic that one of the land use practices that's largely
to blame for bleeding that river dry, namely agriculture, has
also provided an alternate food source. Today the cranes
feed on waste grain for the bulk of their diet, and the farmers don't mind because the birds mainly take what the cattle

leave behind. But they still need the protein and minerals that are essential for successful reproduction, and can only get that from the few marshes that are left. Protein in the form of invertebrates such as worms, snails, and grubs, and minerals, especially calcium, in the form of precipitates."

We were beginning to see cranes in the cornfields again. A flock passed high overhead, navigating unseen currents. Howard leaned over the steering wheel and looked up through the windshield, straining to get a better view.

"They say that the crane formations were the inspiration for Mercury when he made up the Greek alphabet."

According to Howard, the birds left the river at sunrise to feed in the fields until about ten in the morning, then retired to more secluded areas and lazed away the day until mid-afternoon, when they again foraged until returning to their river roost around sunset.

"We can't afford to lose any more of those wetlands—not if we have any sense of responsibility to these birds."

And a host of other species, plant and animal. The tone of his voice was more serious.

"We're on the edge now, maybe past the edge." Howard gave the impression that his own fate was tied to that of the cranes, which in a way maybe it is.

"Of course, if they keep bleeding the river, it won't matter anyway. Good Lord."

It was the Platte that pointed the way west for hundreds of thousands of migrants in the middle of the last century, searching for their individual and collective Manifest Destiny. Since then, "the great lost river" has undergone a number of profound transformations. More than forty dams were built in the Platte River Basin, mainly on the North

Platte and the mainstem, and this resulted in an 80 percent reduction in flows from presettlement days.

I was acquainted with the type of changes that more than a half-century of building dams and water diversions can cause. A few years back, I worked with some folks at the University of Wyoming on a cooperative research project that focused on the changes along the North Platte, changes caused primarily by the construction of five major reservoirs starting with Pathfinder, completed in 1909, and ending with Glendo in 1957.

Throughout the Platte River Basin, the sequence of events was essentially the same. With large reductions in both peak and annual flows, the river narrowed and cottonwoods invaded the former channel. Historically, snow-melt in the Rockies resulted in large floods that prevented seedlings from becoming established. Early explorers and settlers described the Platte River as a mile (1.6 kilometers) wide, an inch (2.5 centimeters) deep, and virtually treeless. Spring meltwater carried large amounts of sediment downstream, leading one traveler to remark that the Platte was "too thick to drink and too thin to plow." These large sediment loads gave the Platte a braided character, with multiple channels that were continually shifting and redefining themselves.

But the floods were controlled now, the river much narrower and deeper, and the grassy banks had become a cottonwood-lined corridor across the Great Plains. This corridor permitted the eastern and western faunas, formerly isolated by the barrier of the "Great American Desert," to mix and in some cases to hybridize.

Of course, without floods, many of the gallery forests are gradually dying out because cottonwood seedlings need open patches with water near the surface in order to reproduce. Sediment deposited by the high flows used to serve this purpose. Today, some scientists speculate that the Russian olive, an exotic tree that escaped cultivation and is now colonizing riparian areas throughout the West, will eventually replace the cottonwood as the climax vegetation on the Platte.

Howard explained that the narrowing of the Platte and the encroachment of vegetation caused the cranes to abandon large reaches of the river.

"They roost on sandbars in shallow water, but only where the channel's wide and only where the vista is unobstructed, giving them a sense of security. Careless species don't generally hang around for 60 million years.

Fewer sandbars are created now because of the reduced flows, the incising of the channel, and because the dams trap most of the sediment. Many of the remaining sandbars are being colonized by cottonwood and willows.

The eighty-mile (130-kilometer) stretch of the Big Bend between Overton and Grand Island remains viable for the birds because of the intensive efforts of groups such as the Audubon Society and the Platte River Whooping Crane Trust. These organizations have purchased approximately 10,000 acres (4,000 hectares) of critical riparian habitat. They mechanically clear the sandbars and attempt to minimize disturbance by limiting human access.

Still, as the cranes are forced to crowd into progressively smaller portions of the river, the changes of the population being drastically reduced by a natural disaster, such as a tornado, or by disease, such as avian cholera, increase greatly. All the while, new plans are being devised for even more impoundments and more diversions, for ways to turn a profit with river water.

"A perforated artery in need of a tourniquet. What kind of a society wants rivers with no water? Good Lord."

· III ·

Our ability to perceive quality in nature begins, as in art, with the pretty. It expands through successive stages of the beautiful to values as yet uncaptured by language. The quality of cranes lies, I think, in this higher gamut, as yet beyond the reach of words.

ALDO LEOPOLD, *A Sand County Almanac*

I crawled out of the blind and joined Drew sitting in the tall grass and milkweed. I figured that "Drew" was short for something, but for the life of me I couldn't figure out what. She taught at the local middle school and seemed to approach life with a certain wide-eyed curiosity and enthusiasm that, while certainly not limited to teachers, is usually found in the good ones. She was in her early forties and a handsome woman, possessing the type of beauty and self-confidence that neither youth nor plastic surgery can provide. I hoped that Howard realized how damn lucky he was.

We could hear the cranes gathering in the nearby fields but none were coming to the river just yet. We sat quietly. The sun was very low now, giving the Johnson grass a beautiful crimson glow. The Platte was calm and suddenly I was feeling quite fortunate. Fortunate to be in this place, at this time, and with these good people. A dozen cranes passed over the cottonwoods and glided down to the river, just downstream from the blind. Howard poked his head out and motioned for us to join him. The show was about to begin.

The blind was small but well built, as I would expect from my capable friend. It was partially excavated so that, while an adult could stand comfortably inside, only the upper half of the structure was above ground. A plywood pentagon on a concrete slab, maybe sixty square feet (six square meters) in all, with three sides affording a view of the river. One for each of us.

The sun was gone now and light was quickly fading. Here and there, small groups of cranes landed on sandbars, nearby. We could see them, silhouettes in the twilight, tall and graceful, long necks turning this way and that, wary and watchful. More and more flocks began to speckle the sky. One after another, they passed. Some landed in this stretch of the river, while others moved downstream. No one spoke, except for an occasional "Good Lord" from Howard. How many times had he witnessed this spectacle? Dozens? Hundreds? Still, he reacted as though it were the first.

The river was beginning to get crowded. Howard said that there might be 15,000 to 20,000 birds in this stretch before it was all said and done—a typical roosting flock. The sky was now filled with sandhill cranes. Line after line, in all directions, as far as the eye could see. An infinite variety of formations, all with a common destination after a day of foraging—the Platte River. The din from the river was rising in intensity and the trumpeting was deafening. The birds were packed in, separated from one another by only a few feet. Not much space—in addition to being the oldest avian species, the sandhill crane is also one of North America's largest, up to four feet (one meter) tall with a six-foot (two-meter) wingspan. While standing on submerged sandbars with those long spindly legs, the cranes gave the appearance of walking on water as the congregation stretched across the entire channel.

It was nearly dark. Surely this night invasion must be nearing completion. I scanned the sky, straining and squinting to see in the fading light. Nothing had changed. The numbers of incoming flocks had not diminished and, according to Howard, probably wouldn't for a while yet. I felt that I was sharing an experience with others who had gone before. The Pawnee and Sioux with their wild ponies and sun-bleached teepees. The early trappers from Cincinnati and St. Louis, who told of bison herds from horizon to horizon. The pioneering naturalist Audubon, who wrote of endless processions of passenger pigeons, a single flock darkening the skies for three days; he painted these doomed birds as he painted the doomed grizzlies and wolves of the grasslands. The Conestoga trekkers of the Oregon Trail, whose wagons took up to two weeks to pass a single prairie dog town. Exaggeration and hyperbole? Who can say? As for the cranes, well, I've seen them for myself.

But numbers alone don't guarantee a future. In North America, we've demonstrated this time and time again, reducing the world's largest animal assemblages, rivaling any in history, to mere curiosities—or worse. Our powers, fantastic; our foresight, limited.

As we left the blind, silent in the cool darkness, I thought of the future. Of the Platte, of crane watchers yet unborn.

I thought of sandhill cranes, a miraculously long thread in the fabric of time. Their comings and goings, as Aldo Leopold wrote with characteristic eloquence, are "the ticking of the geologic clock."

We live in a society that's increasingly rootless; fewer and fewer walk in the footsteps of their father or their father's father. In such a world, the spectacle of uncountable numbers of cranes has the capacity to bind generations together, to remind us of what we have in common, rather than what we can count as yours or mine. If we could ever reach beyond trickle-down and trickle-out economics, see beyond our own pathetically short lives, maybe we could rediscover a piece of the lost river, and in the process find something that we've lost in ourselves.

It was nearly midnight. As I climbed into the truck cab, the sound of thousands of cranes voicing that now-familiar ratchety trill echoed loudly in the night air and drowned out the serious little voice in my head. Good Lord.

A MAP *for* HUMMINGBIRDS

. . . .

(ELLEN MELOY)

MONTANA'S WILD geese migrate in family units. They navigate by memory and topography—the shape of a mountain, a curve of river—and by an internal compass that responds to the earth's magnetic field. The point bird in the distinctive v-shaped formation is usually a gander, although the geese change position frequently. Updrafts of air behind each wing in the v reduce drag for all but the leader, which must drop back to rest. Think of the v as a single creature: aerodynamically fluid and energy efficient, adjusting its flight pattern by loud honks.

Borne by sturdy bodies and powerful wings, the geese stay aloft for hours. The peoples of old did not underestimate the endurance of migratory birds with large body mass. They also observed, correctly, that hummingbirds migrate but presumed that such tenderly small creatures—birds that must eat constantly to fuel a rapid-fire heartbeat—could not fly long distances on their own without dropping dead. Thus, according to folk belief, big Canada geese would carry tiny, fragile, hitchhiking hummingbirds on their backs when they migrated.

A cold front can trigger migration in the fall, although the precise moment of departure is never predictable. Not all goose families are of like mind about staying or leaving or when. One minute they might be nibbling succulent plant bits in a serene valley, the next minute they rise into the clean blue air above the Montana-Idaho border. Below lies a rumpled cordillera of rocks and ice and a pickup winding along the Interstate highway. Inside the truck are two humans, also migrants, also at odds about staying or leaving or when. Cranked on for the first time in months, the truck heater smells like melting chihuahuas. The man drives. The woman, who never wears socks south of Pocatello, takes off her battered desert sandals, pulls on a pair of woolies and shoes, then stares down at her feet as if they were freshly embalmed mummies. Paths cross. The distance between sky and road, wing and tire, diminishes sound but not a vague sense of air flowing in opposite directions. The southbound geese comb our northbound hair.

Birds respond to changes in their environment by migrating. In temperate North America the best strategy is to move south for the winter to warmer terrain, where better menus flourish, and to return north in the spring, where the mild season and longer daylight hours favor mating, nesting, feeding, and growing up. Nature, of course, never quite sticks to the grid. Some birds head south when they should head north. My ornithology book defines reverse migration as bird movement that proceeds in the direction opposite the one expected for the season. If a storm or heavy winds sweep them off course, for instance, the birds fly back to the beginning or to a point where instinct reorients them to their preferred lane of passage.

Reverse migration is the metaphor of my life in Montana. My husband's seasonal work as a backcountry ranger and a home we built in southern Utah keep us in the desert during the hottest months, from early spring until late fall. Our slightly delirious Utah life, spent largely outdoors, unfolds in the sensuous red-gold light of a heat-scorched, tense, skinless earth fissured with deep canyons and upthrust in sandstone monoliths. Each winter I haul my lizard pelt and desert soul back to our Montana home, blue-starved. For months I have not seen so much light at this end of the spectrum: thick conifer forests the color of malachite, steel-gray peaks creased with cobalt shadows, lofty cornices underlined with blue-violet cusps of snow. Montana is a sojourn in northern light.

The truck moves through an indigo dark. The geese push onward to open water and a rest. At this point in our migration all other vehicles have fallen off Idaho, whose edge meets an abyss into outer space—or so it seems. Our vehicle slips solo up the massive plateau that hovers above the rest of the continent like Coleridge's Xanadu ("That sunny dome! those caves of ice!"), a distant, glittering place undercut by something dark and alluring. The night beyond our high beams obliterates all horizons, all distinction between land and sky. The lights of scattered ranches become stars. Nothing but the ground beneath me tells me that gravity exists. Away from towns spread like islands in Montana's vast space, few travelers are immune to the floating sensation caused by this blanket of darkness.

Geographers often describe Montana's size with the how-many-states-can-fit-into-it measure. Nearly three Connecticuts. A couple of Vermonts. One slightly distended West Virginia. Stretch the analogy further: overlay Massachusetts onto southwestern Montana, where I live. The Crazy Mountains impale Boston, tossing half a million people downslope into a rude heap. Cape Cod's curled finger tickles a paltry number of sage-freckled acres west of Twodot, and the Connecticut River disappears into the Missouri like a lost noodle. The Berkshire Hills form a dust cover to the Scapegoat Wilderness. Cowboys from Deer Lodge sell Housatonic gentry a few sizable cattle outfits. The city of Butte pierces the overlay, startling everyone in New Bedford with a giant open-pit copper mine. Yellowstone National Park, however, now sits conveniently in their backyard.

Montana easily fits Gertrude Stein's remark, "more space where nobody is than where anybody is." The journalist Joseph Kinsey Howard called Montana "the space between people," implying that a vehicle and a few tanks of gas are needed merely to bring you close enough to see if the other person's eyes are blue or brown. So much space fosters deep introspection, philosophic distraction, fierce independence, and narrative inventiveness—desirable traits for writers, cowboys, and that up-and-coming New West prodigy, the golf pro. Under the Big Sky, human and landscape exist in the right proportion to one another; comfort is found in one's own insignificance. As a young, insignificant woman I believed that Montana's humbling and informing scale would provide the proper vessel for my terminal restlessness, my notion that home could be found in movement itself. I felt that rootlessness might find root in a place of this size.

Some birds, notably young gulls, herons, and egrets, do not always migrate in predictable seasonal directions. Juvenile wandering can be linear—the young birds head north as the rest of the colony heads south—or explosive: they move in all directions and at considerable distances from their hatching area. When immature birds cannot compete successfully for food with older birds, they must wander until they find an adequate food supply for themselves.

Years ago I came to Montana as a juvenile wanderer, a native westerner exchanging one rural home for another. Behind me I dragged previous lives—student, lifeguard, hermit—and ahead lay a buffet of new ones. I made a living in technical illustration, churning out laboriously stippled pen-and-inks of bones and feathers, detailed diagrams of geological strata, and the cell divisions of anxious amoebas. The medium enriched my knowledge of science and gave me thumb calluses, thick reading glasses, and the revelation that my art, so meticulous in nature, was also extremely uptight. For relief I painted barns.

In the Rockies' brief growing season I jump-started my garden inside a junked farm truck, its cab and windshield facing south, its windows adjusted for ventilation. This greenhouse yielded seedlings for tons of unlikely tomatillos and one cantaloupe the size and flavor of a used tennis ball. Montana's weather crossed Seattle with the Yukon: one storm covered the land in humid, brooding skies, the next in brittle, frigid air that burned the skin like poisoned needles. Contrary to predictions, winter didn't kill me. I boldly crawled under the house to thaw my pipes with a blow dryer.

When a more severe cold snap froze every molecule of liquid in my house except a tumbler of whiskey, I drank the whiskey. I survived winter's cold but not its length; each year I fled to the desert to cheat it.

In Montana I married a man who called his sleeping bag "Doris" and lived three blocks from where he was born. At the time of his birth, in the early fifties, the neighborhood boasted a hospital, a convent, modest family homes, and one active and at least five former brothels. On one of our first dates he took me to a bird refuge in a remote intermontane valley, where he shot a duck and served me its tiny butchered breasts for dinner. Before I could decide how I felt about dead duck, he told me its name: bufflehead. We were eating bufflehead breasts.

In Montana I learned to fly-fish, row a river raft, belly dance, and herd sheep. I frost-nipped my feet on cross-country ski trips in moonlight and rearranged my knee cartilage on treks across mountains with a heavy pack. The land seemed so vast, each season so deep, adventure became irresistible, even if moments of exquisite beauty had to be earned by extreme pain. These years matched youth to place, reckless energy to a land that does not yield easy living to anyone.

Perhaps the southbound geese that flew above our northbound heads picture their winter grounds as an enormous open-air restaurant; their primary occupation is to eat. On my feeding grounds on the upper Missouri River, I exchange the lusty, brainless, overheated, intimately physical life of the desert for winter's distinct mood of reflection. I trade summer's harlotry of color for what Melville called a "fixed trance of whiteness." I trade the wild for shelter.

My street abuts a million acres of timbered high country along the Continental Divide, possibly the last street until the next town nearly ninety miles (145 kilometers) away. Here, edge of town means a distinct, palpable border. On the tamed side of the wilderness, below our house, lies the old redlight quarter and, wedged into a narrow gulch, a dense cluster of commercial buildings with ornate facades of sandstone and granite. Montana's innards—gold, silver, copper, lead—paid the bill and fed the town's aspirations to worldliness. A delirious mix of architectural elements borrowed from the Italian Romanesque, French Renaissance, midwestern American Gothic, and mining-camp Baroque doesn't quite hide a frontier soul. Similar opulence is found on the downtown's other flank, merely a gulch away from the whorehouses, in a neighborhood of stately mansions built at the turn of the century by mining magnates who followed a cardinal rule: The dirtier your mine, the farther you live from it. They lived here, close to their banks.

What could be more western than an endemic confusion of virtues? As towns like mine outgrew their frontier motleyness, civic pride called for churches, schools, and other refinements. Visitors from the East wanted mud and bugling elk and virile men who mumbled about posses and punched each other's lights out. As the nation paved its highways in the thirties, Montana, short on funds and long on need, stretched its blacktop budget by building its highways as narrow as possible. Not that it mattered; traffic was negligible and everyone drove all over both lanes anyway. These days *los ombres de global economy* dress like Wyatt Earp on weekends but demand a four-lane to the ski lift. Everyone wants Montana to be not a state but a state of mind.

The downtown district recently sprouted a thick crop of espresso bars. From my house I can walk this gauntlet and arrive overcaffeinated at my favorite bookstore. The cafes, and weekly calls from realtors hoping to wrest our house from us, portend Montana's demise as a faraway, hostile, possibly coffeeless place. The great interior West is filling. Hoarding the limelight are white supremacists, golf pros, a ranch-hungry Hollywood elite, and nearly everyone else from California who saw the flyfishing movie. The state's soul, however, perches precariously between pieces of its own myth as a paradise of raw nature and a backwater of rural primitives in love with sheep and assault rifles.

In winter Montanans become a hearth people, content to shut the door against the howling wilderness. The season exacerbates an insularity in the Montana character, an ease with keeping to oneself without diminishing one's community. A few cope by shooting their refrigerators. Others embrace the pleasure, if not the necessity, of friends and neighbors, one of whom might someday pluck them from a snowdrift. Ranches a tenth the size of Belgium keep a lot of people far apart. Early homesteaders often built their houses on adjacent corners of their sections and lived close to one another. Before long they moved to the other side of their holding, ostensibly because their chickens got mixed up together. Something about this extraordinary land accommodates a desire for privacy without loneliness, seclusion without solitude.

The winter solstice marks the midpoint of our stay in the far North. This calendar suspends me in the purity of a singular season; winter's most evocative qualities freeze-frame in a landscape that wears them to perfection. Days

unfold in preternaturally bright sunlight or under a pewter
sky weighted against snowy hills with its impending storm.
Nights are sudden and complete, with a faint glacial scent.
The moon is lilac as it rises, silver at its zenith. I never see
the seasons change in Montana, I never see the green, only
its scheduled death. For me Montana is always cold, the
original and ultimate state of the universe.

January brings the coldest days, bone-chilling polar air
that leaves no slack. Every surface freezes so hard it would
rip your lips off if you kissed it. Car exhausts spew dry-ice
fumes. The air crackles with helium, ozone, neon, argon—
air that can be 108 degrees colder than me—yet somehow
I remain liquid. Not counting my bathtub, the aquariums
in the local pet store have the only open water for miles.
Winter's worst grip sends me there for the solace of gurgling
water and a fecund, tidal humidity. The same Arctic front
sends the derelicts to the library. Some sit cozily next to
the heat vent in their baggy parkas and unlaced pac boots.
Another sleeps at a table, snoring face down on *La Technique: Cooking with Jacques Pepin.*

Despite the pervasive lethargy of hibernation, things
get done. Ravenously hungry after the cold spell, cedar
waxwings—tawny birds with black bands across their eyes—
strip my crabapple tree of its frozen fruit, then fly off like
masked bandits. My husband cleans the basement. Someone
resuscitates all those Bostonians heaped at the foot of the
Crazies. According to the news, the Romanians are selling
their excess bears. I order two. The legislature, which meets
here every two years for ninety days, undoes the laws that
the previous session repassed in response to laws depassed by
the session before that, making everyone so dizzy, we wish

they would meet every ninety years for two days. I send out postcards with photos of typical Rocky Mountain ungulates and letters that note a ski trip to the valley of the bufflehead breasts, the length of icicles, the blizzards and the chinooks, the shock of exploding color from arriving seed catalogues, an epidemic of imploding marriages among friends—all the riches and wrecks that mark life as *Homo sapiens* on a wobbly, spinning planet that tilts its northern hemisphere away from the sun.

Then the season turns and the light slowly climbs the orb.

Before migrating a bird must eat a great deal, storing energy in the form of subcutaneous fat. The bird must also become predisposed to migrate by a metabolic state called migratory restlessness. In spring this condition is controlled by the pituitary gland, which in turn is stimulated by periodicity, or changes in day length. Fat, restless, and physiologically prepared, the bird now needs only the external stimulus of a drop in barometric pressure, the moist, southerly air of a warm front, before it loads those little hummingbirds on its back and takes wing: northbound.

For me the migratory impulse manifests itself in too many trips to the pet store aquariums. The geography wars, the tension between allegiances to two places, escalate. One day I will press my face against a window that frames Montana's crystalline winter purity and I, too, will long for hummingbirds. Fat, restless, and physiologically prepared, aching for the desert, I will turn winter's bend with the geese and take wing: southbound.

THE NAMING *of* PARTS

. . . .

(RICHARD MABEY)

And this you can see is the bolt. The purpose of this
Is to open the breech, as you can see. We can slide it
Rapidly backwards and forwards: We call this
Teasing the spring. And rapidly backwards and forwards
The early bees are assaulting and fumbling the flowers:
They call it easing the Spring.

from "The Naming of Parts" by HENRY REED, 1941

IT MUST be spring. The gale has switched to the southwest,
and it's hard to walk upright. In the brief glints of sun,
the guinea-pigs press themselves against the wire-mesh of
their cage, braving the wind for a few minutes of warmth. It
is all I can do not to set them free. The cats have gone back
to lounging in my room, the one island of warmth in the

house. When Blanco, always the outdoor boy, comes back through the cat-flap like a meteor, I look out of the window, and see a big dog fox trying to get in, too. His fur is standing on end, as if he had been the one who'd been shocked.

The war blunders on, and rattled by the weather as well as fears of terrorist reprisals, the countryside has gone into siege mode. The supermarkets have put bottled water on ration. Our DIY store has sold out of masking tape, which seems to have become a kind of talisman, believed to have the power to ward off unmentionable plagues. What a hope. An archeologist friend excavating the remains of a medieval hospital in Scotland (the scene of earlier tribal wars) tells me he has found anthrax spores still viable after six hundred years. And every village has just one house with a Union Jack in the garden.

But the plants are indomitable. The "blackthorn winter" starts in the second week of April, frosting the hedges while the wild plums are still in blossom. I'm finding flowers and flourishes that are quite new to me. Down in the fen there are the beginnings of things that I can't hope to identify: the first thin spikes of sedges, the russet spears of leaves not yet touched by chlorophyll, finials of the peat. There are precocious cowslips everywhere—on roadsides, churchyards, uncut back lawns. One patch is growing with luminous blue ground-ivy on a dead log—an extraordinary color combination. Something has happened, some subtle change in climate or soil chemistry, to help the cowslips back. There are newcomers, too. The first big wayside flower of the year here is the white comfrey. It's only been "loose" here a couple of centuries, naturalized from Turkey, but its starched-linen, wine-goblet flowers are as cheering as snowdrops—which are still in flower, too, three months on from their first appearance.

But I am bothered about the migrants. I haven't heard a willow warbler or a blackcap, normally in full chorus by early April. Not a single passing swallow has hinted at a change in the seasons, and I worry again about the ominously expanding deserts and blighted marshes of the Middle East, through which so many of Norfolk's summer visitors must pass. But in the house we get things ready for them. The barn doors are left open. The windows near where the house martins nest are shut. Kate puts up a painting of a martlet just inches away from the back of their last year's mud-shell. We wait—and on the date the cuckoos should have arrived, the West ousts Saddam.

. . .

IN THE mizzling weather I take to walking in the dusk. I suspect there's a trace of asceticism in this, a desire to confront the awful sterility of East Anglia's farming landscape head-on; and maybe, too, a sulky determination to make the worst of this seemingly endless false start, to not see what is not yet there. The dark strips things down, lays them bare in the same way that snow does. All the ornamentations of the daytime, the frills and spurts of spring, are clouded, and you are left with the basic imperatives of geology and weather. And in a ruthlessly agricultural landscape like East Anglia, with the contours of power. In the half-light the edges of the lanes melt away, and the remains of the hedgebanks and ditches that were created two thousand years ago now seem little more than parentheses round the fields. The few patches of woodland, kept for pheasants, are indistinguishable in silhouette from the battery farms devoted to another ex-Asian game bird—except that the low forcing-sheds glow dimly from twenty-four-hour lighting systems designed to ensure the chickens stay awake, fattening-up.

Sometimes I catch glimpses of other dusk-hunters: a few spring moths, a late departing woodcock, pipistrelle and long-eared bats, flickering shapes in that brief window between it being too light for them to fly and too dark for me to see. One evening, on Mellis Common, I saw a jack snipe crouched under a molehill, mouse-like and tense. I thought it was a skylark until it jinked off silently into the twilight, bound for its nesting-ground in the Arctic. We were ships passing in the night.

But so much that was once part of the experience of the April dusk, even in my childhood, seems to be missing. The gnat swarms are smaller, the chorusing blackbirds fewer. Most painfully of all, there are no barn owls. I've heard rumors of one that haunts the western reaches of the valley, but in six months haven't seen a single bird within 20 miles (about 30 kilometers). Up till fifty years ago they'd been parish familiars throughout England, keeping their pale vigil over the pastures. When I was a child a pair had nested in a barn not more than 300 yards (275 meters) from my house, and their hunting range matched up almost exactly with the boundaries of our gang's territory in the Field: over the old brick piles that were all that remained of the Hall, up the ivy-clad wall that lined the council estate, across the steep field we used for tobogganing, then down, if we were lucky, through the bosky edges of our back gardens. The memory of the owls beating past the poplar trees—burnished golden wings against lime-green leaves in the evening light—is one of the few visual images of childhood I can recall with absolute clarity. Now I see the white owl not so much as an object in the landscape but as a creature looking at me. It is an uncompromising gaze: this is *me,* it says, on my estate, about my business. What's yours? No wonder barn owls were seen as guardian spirits, beaters of the bounds between humans and the wild.

Their image has always been an ambivalent one. The tawny owl's generic name is *Strix,* Latin for witch, and there are stories of the Church burning owls for witchcraft in the Middle Ages. Yet in the countryside barn owls (from a related family) were also white witches, symbols of luck and continuity, and farmers would nail owl corpses to barn doors to frighten off evil spirits. In eighteenth-century Selborne they nested under the eaves of the parish church, and Gilbert White noted how they had adjusted their hunting flights to the architecture: as "feet are necessary in their ascent under the tiles, they constantly perch first on the roof of the chancel, and shift the mouse from their claws to their bill, that the feet may be at liberty to take hold of the plate on the wall as they are rising under the eaves." One of White's friends in Wiltshire told him about "a vast hollow pollard-ash that had been the mansion of owls for centuries." He'd found a congealed mass that turned out to be "a congerie of the bones of mice (and perhaps of birds and bats) that had been heaping together for ages, being cast up in the pellets out of the crops of many generations of inhabitants."

Seventy-five years later John Clare, adrift in his asylum, remembered the normalcy, the neighborliness of the parish owl:

Now the owl on wheaten wing
And white hood scowling o'er his eyes,
Jerking with a sudden spring
Through the three-cornered barn holes flies.

from "Evening," written on 14 February 1847

In the early years of the twentieth century they were still hovering in some borderland between the familiar and the mysterious. The transactions of the Norfolk Naturalists Trust carried an extraordinary account of a pair seen in February not far from this valley, and seeming to the observer to be "luminous." There was a light mist in the air, and they were floating like will-o'-the-wisps over a patch of marshy ground. One "emerged from a covert about 200 yards distant, flying backwards and forwards across the field, at times approaching within 50 yards of where I was standing... It literally lit up the branches of the trees as it flew past." The owls had probably picked up phosphorescence from roosting in the crumbling "touchwood" of trees smitten with honey fungus. Yet they were an eerie enough sight to convince one Norfolk naturalist that they had the power to generate their own illumination. Barn owls are creatures not just of the geographical margins but the cultural margins, too, of the debatable ground.

In East Anglia they call unkempt and unresolved corners of land "muddles"; and it was the post-war un-muddling of the landscape, the concerted drive towards tidiness and efficiency, that marked the turning-point for the barn owl. Almost everywhere the green lanes and road verges were overmown and drenched with chemicals. The pastures were converted to arable and the stackyards to silos. The barns themselves were flattened, or made into smart houses. Many of the owls were flattened, too, hunting along old routeways that had suddenly become major roads. By the 1990s the U.K. population was down to less than five thousand pairs, about a third of the numbers half a century before. And about that time there was an uncanny rerun of the excavation Gilbert White had reported in the 1770s. Less than a mile (about a kilometer) from White's village, an old chimney stack was opened for the first time since it was capped in 1913. Inside were three sackfuls of perfectly preserved and desiccated barn owl pellets. They revealed an immense variety of diet. Among eight hundred identifiable food items were fourteen species of mammal—including water shrew, Natterer's bat, weasel, and dormouse—fragments of frogs, swallows, yellowhammers, and an abundance of insects. Nothing like this variety has ever been found in modern barn owl pellets, and these relics, preserved in their original site like fossils, were a reminder of the diversity of the countryside before the Great War.

What is one to make of the decline of the screech owl—Norfolk's Billy Wise, Yorkshire's Jenny Howler, Sussex's Moggy—a passing perhaps unmourned by the increasing numbers of people who have never seen one in the wild? Few birds are so dramatically beautiful, or can bring the exquisite delicacy of flight so close to us, or can look at us so penetratingly, eye to eye. But they mean more than that. Ecologists look to the condition of "top predators" as a measure of how well they ecosystem on which they depend is working. The barn owl is a cultural indicator, too. We recognize, at a deep level, the meaning of that ritual crossing of the fields. It is a sacrament, a consecration of "good ground" and the boundaries between light and dark, of the proper order of things. Just as the summer migrants stand for renewal, so the barn owl stands for continuity, and its passing leaves us that bit less grounded.

. . .

BUT INSIDIOUSLY, teasingly, the migrants began to flit into the valley. It was like the eddying of a piece of gossip—"There's news! We're back!"—first in one village, then the next, then back again with a new twist.

15 April: Kestrels and sparrowhawks are doing display fights high above the meadow. I surprise two kestrels in the barn, above a little mound of vole-fur pellets. Later that day, there are three swallows on a wire at Dickleburgh, 6 miles (about 10 kilometers) away.

16 April: A beautiful, hot day, after a light frost. The wild cherry is in bloom, and I see one swallow at a farm half a mile (less than 1 kilometer) up the road. The cats are suffused with the rising sap. On my bed, just after dawn, Blackie stretches theatrically out in front of Lily, asking to be washed. Lily obliges, nibbling her face and neck to do the job properly. From the other side of the bed Blanco watches intently. His head is jutting forward, in a tense posture that usually means jealousy, or peevishness. I think he's going to pounce. But he pads slowly towards Blackie and Lily until he's about 6 inches (15 centimeters) away. Never dropping his stare, he begins flexing his back legs up and down, in the same kneading action that cats use when doing "contentments" with their front paws. He has an orgasm with a small curdled cry, then pads back to his side of the bed, washes his willy, and goes to sleep. Outside, somewhere on the far side of the Ling, the first cuckoo calls.

17 April: Still fine and warm. I slip into the grounds of the big house to see if there are swallows and martins over the lake. There aren't, but four little gulls, *en route* from the Mediterranean to the Baltic, are wafting over the water, the reflection of their black underwings rippling on the surface. Later, I go down to the little fen at Roydon. This is an improbable oasis, 40 acres (16 hectares) of swamp and carr within sight and sound of the main road to Diss. Things are showing: the first quill spikes of reeds, the fretwork leaves of meadow-rue, and deep among the alders, sheaves of yellow iris blades. I try to stop prying so anxiously, to relax my ears, let the place wash over me. The fen feels as if it has been hung up to dry in the sun. Last year's sedges look parched, as if it were the end of summer, not the beginning. A tree-creeper appears at the foot of a willow, jerks up the trunk, probing the crevices with its bodkin bill, then swoops down to the foot of the next tree, "weaving the wood together" in Paul Evans's words. The greenery is burgeoning. There are plants in their aboriginal home here that I only know as hedgerow oddities. Wild hops are shooting out of patches of damp loam, often yards from any support, and beginning to twine up flag blades, tussocks, even each other. Native red-currants are growing in pools and flashes of stagnant water. Their young leaves have a purple sheen, as if they have been dabbed with wine, and the first tassels of yellow-green flowers, five-petaled, have the look of tiny medieval carvings.

The fen is full of more humdrum plants, too—nettle, woody nightshade, the asparagus-like shoots of horsetail. Fenland's intrinsic shiftiness and changeability have made it one of the foundries of the vegetation of disturbed ground, and the species that evolved in its oozes of silt are among those that have found congenial homes in the mud of farmyards and the rich loams of vegetable gardens.

I walk on into the fen. Somewhere above me I hear a snatch of a muted, thrush-like song, and see a bird fly up to the top of an alder. But it's not a song-thrush. It has a dark eye-stripe, and through binoculars I can see it's a redwing. Another joins it, and they sit stock-still, looking south. Then the new bird turns slowly round to gaze at the singer. It underwing covers show with the same warm russet colors as the alder buds. Is the urge to fly back to Scandinavia stirring in them? Or is the perfection of the light and warmth, the imminent leafing, making them pause? What does it take to make a bird override the hard-wiring that determines migration? Pulled by two contrary instincts, to settle and migrate, would they experience the anxiety of choice? Redwings have bred in England, in Kent, and stayed deep into the summer in Suffolk. In the Chilterns, on almost the same date as today, I once saw a departing redwing in the same hedge as a newly arrived redstart. Redstart, redwing, red-budded tree, redcurrant: so many messages from the shade. But when the redwings flew off the spring fen fell silent, and I thought uncomfortably of Rachel Carson's prophetic book.

18 April: At 9 AM there is a flash of white rump and a snatch of bony chatter outside my window. A single house-martin swoops up to one of last year's nests, clings to the shell, then flies away as abruptly as it arrived.

BUT THE migrant birds still seemed elusive and sparse. The swallows of a few weeks before had deserted the farms. I hadn't heard the shrill flutings of the blackcaps that should have been abundant in the fens, or for that matter that first herald of spring, a chiffchaff. Had they been disorientated, too, blown off their traditional route-ways by Mediterranean storms? My nightmare, that those ancient ecological links with the south might finally be broken, wouldn't go away. And, as usual at such times, I whirled about, looking for reassurance. I went over to the Suffolk coast, and heard a single nightingale. I pestered friends, who all seemed to be seeing and hearing more than me. I phoned up Bird-lines, Migrant Watch-lines, and heard that, yes, there was a weather block over the continent slowing movement down, but the birds were coming through. And I began to won-der if it was me, as much as them, that was "blocked." My hearing had been deteriorating for the past decade, and I had to face up to the possibility that I had lost most of the high-pitched warbler songs, just as I had lost the screaming of swifts. It wasn't a pleasant prospect, being cut off from the one thing that made me feel *not* cut off. Gilbert White had bouts of deafness in middle age, so that he lost "all the pleasing notices and little intimations arising from rural sounds." "And Wisdom," he quoted at the end of a letter, "at one entrance quite shut out."

That late April Polly and I went over to the Broads again, to see our friends Mary and Mark Cocker. Mark is an envi-ably acute man, as sharp in the field as he is in his writing, and I knew that a walk with him would settle things. We make up a bit of a mixed flock, three adults, Mark's eight-year-old daughter Miriam, and a neighbor's son, Kevin, who has insisted on tagging along. We walk along the River Chat, by reed-fringed ditches and clumps of willow scrub. The water flashes intermittently a few paces away. Mark spots sand martins while I'm peering at the ground. He picks up the whiplash song of a Cettis warbler, something I know well and was sure I was capable of hearing. He seems able to conjure birds out of thin air. Then, smartingly, he spots swifts high up over the mere we're walking towards. This is not how I wanted to see my first birds of the year— my first proper swifts since I'd been ill—pointed out for me while I'm looking the other way. I feel humiliated, and hurt, as if I had had a personal gift unwrapped for me. The birds were here, and I was simply failing to register them. Was my hearing even dodgier than I thought? Was my attention still on that wall that I gazed at for so long?

I watch Mark. He's standing upright, scanning forwards, but still holding hands with Miri and talking to her. He calls out terns, a marsh harrier, more martins, which I'm simply not picking up. So I watch myself, too. I'm conscious of the fact that my mind is constantly drifting. My eyes are pointed downwards, focused on some important spot of ground about 5 feet (1.5 meters) in front of me, a crass compromise between staring nervously at one's feet and navigating forward. It's a botanist's stance, but a depressive's hunch, too. Birders use the jargon word "dipping" for failing to see rarities, and it seemed a peculiarly apt metaphor for me at that moment.

Kevin, meanwhile, arms akimbo, is talking gibberish about computer games. He hurls stones at the water, drops the binoculars I've lent him, tears up handfuls of reeds, nearly falls in. He's got attention-deficit syndrome. Miri shakes her head at him, and tells me about her elder sister Rachel's forthcoming appearance in the school production of *Wind in the Willows*. She's playing a weasel, and Miri makes the battle for Toad Hall sound like a piece of woodland agitprop, as the oppressed creatures storm the seat of privilege. I think I'm suffering from attention deficit too. I'm projecting my own debility onto the natural world, in a bizarre physiological version of the pathetic fallacy (that tendency among the Romantics to see human emotions reflected in the workings of nature). The migrants may be late, and down in numbers, but it's me that's really missing the boat, and the cues.

The frustration and sense of loss—how many more springs had I got left?—drove me into a rare bout of technological busyness. I could do something about my attention, but for my hearing I needed help, some clever escape route out of my personal silent spring. I went to see my audiologist, who denied there was anything superior to my hearing aid. I thought of the ear-trumpet that was among Gilbert White's effects, but felt such a thing might be a tad ostentatious for the fens. David Cobham did some lateral thinking and suggested I went to a detective agency, but they informed me that portable devices for tuning in to distant sounds were just so much filmmakers' fiction. So it was down to me, and a handful of specialist electrical shops, and the end-result was a combination of a high-quality directional microphone, a digital voice recorder and a pair of Walkman headphones. I called it Auric. The first time I took it out was a revelation: the birds I thought might be stretched out between Baghdad and the Alps—gassed, starved, gale-wrecked—seemed to be singing exultantly only a few feet away. I heard properly, for the first time since my thirties, the little grace notes in reed warblers' songs, the scratching of whitethroats, and that thin, triumphant *see-saw* of the chiffchaff.

And, paying for that artificial recapturing of youthful senses, I also heard, enormously amplified, the shattering roar of distant aircraft and the hum of traffic. It was, I felt, a fair swap, since these are the realities of the world to which our migrants return. But they'd made it back to where they belonged, and back, too, inside my head.

THE END
OF BIRDS

FLYING *to* VIETNAM

. . . .

(SUSAN BROWNMILLER)

T RAVELERS SHOULD strike out into the unknown even within the context of the unfamiliar. With that in mind, while I was in Vietnam last November, I left Saigon for the Mekong Delta. A cryptic reference in something I'd read offered a promising destination: a bird reserve in the reedy marshland of Dong Thap province that was supposedly a short drive from Cao Lanh.

Who had set up a sanctuary in the delta, and how had they done it, were intriguing questions for me and my travel companion—and for Tuyen, our guide, who was looking for new tourist attractions. Our driver, Thanh, a sober-sided realist who during the war had worked for "You-said" (USAID, the U.S. Agency for International Development), said that the road past Cao Lanh was unpaved and frequently flooded.

Of all the world's rivers that resonate with romance, conquest, fertile plains, warfare, human migration, and suffering, few command more respect than the Mekong, as it flows for 2,600 miles (4,000 kilometers) from the Tibetan highlands through Cambodia and Vietnam to the South China Sea. Laboring peasants turned the alluvial soil of the delta into Vietnam's rice bowl. The patchwork of tributaries, canals, dikes, and irrigation ditches is home to one-quarter of the country's people and sustenance to an additional 25 percent, who rely on its crops, its fisheries, and increasingly, its offshore oil.

During the Vietnam War—to them, the American War—the delta was a Vietcong stronghold, targeted for pacification, search-and-destroy operations, tons of napalm and chemical defoliants, and barbed-wire enclaves called strategic hamlets, which were ours during the day, theirs at night. More recently, refugees from Cambodia and the Khmer Rouge settled in the recovering region, for which no doubt they felt some affinity. On maps drawn before the 18th century, much of the watery land belonged to the Cambodian kingdom.

The sun was shining on the rice fields as we drove along at a leisurely pace, stopping now and again to observe the age-old rhythms of life along the Mekong, where three crops of grain can be harvested a year. We reached the river port of Cao Lanh by lunchtime, staggered by the size of the Soviet-style memorial that was inscribed, typically, THE FATHERLAND WILL NOT FORGET YOU.

After lunch we set off again for the bird reserve. By now it was past 2:00 PM, and the road beyond Cao Lanh was not only unpaved but badly rutted as it stretched toward infinity, lined on both sides with thatch-and-wood houses, sometimes on stilts with a rickety little bridge of logs and branches spanning a muddy stream. On it went: a never-ending village of wall-to-wall humanity with peasants tending to mats of rice drying on the roadside, chickens crossing the path, children playing, women preparing a meal, shirtless men in green army pants, a water buffalo in harness, a cart loaded with pigs, a lactating dog, teams of bicycles, a roaring scooter, a lumbering, freshly painted DeSoto bus bearing the legend DONG THAP, a modest stand selling cigarettes and soda.

When Tuyen would inquire how far to the bird reserve, the answer was always "twenty kilometers on." Once it was "seven kilometers," and we visibly brightened, but then it was "twenty kilometers" again.

It was dark when we reached Tam Nong, a lively settlement in a New Economic Zone, and learned that the bird reserve was across the bridge. We had traveled more than 50 miles (80 kilometers) from Cao Lanh. (We didn't know that it would have been quicker and easier to travel the route by boat.)

Approaching a lighted, substantial house, I groggily wondered if they'd have to take us in. The reserve's director, who greeted us in his pajamas, seemed to be having the same thought. "This happens all the time," he said with a shrug.

The name of the reserve, we learned, was Tram Chim, which means "bird swamp." Tuyen introduced me as an American writer. The director beamed and said something I heard as "Audubon."

"Ah, yes, Audubon," I beamed back.

"You know this name?" asked Tuyen. "The director says he came here four years ago to help set up the sanctuary." That didn't seem right, but I was in no mood to quibble.

We were offered tea after we agreed to return to the nearby town for the night. At 6 AM, if we wished, we could go out in a launch and see Tram Chim, or at least a portion of its 45,000 acres (18,000 hectares). Before we departed for the evening, we were taken to an exhibition room that solved part of the mystery. The name that I had heard was Archibald, not Audubon. Posters of the International Crane Foundation and a picture of cofounder George Archibald were on the wall.

After a restless night in the Tam Nong motel (at some point the karaoke music did stop; at 3 AM I crawled out of the mosquito netting and figured out how to turn off the refrigeration unit), we were ready for the birds.

This was not crane season at the Tram Chim Reserve. The sarus crane—a five-foot (1.5-meter)-tall, redheaded bird—arrives in late December and stays through April, while the painted stork comes by for a shorter visit. But during our three hours in the launch, guided by an earnest young man named Thieng, we saw black drongos, common kingfishers, purple herons, gray herons, great egrets, black-shouldered kites, lapwings, swallows, cormorants, and a purple swamp hen.

Thieng carried a dog-eared copy of *A Guide to the Birds of Thailand* for reference. He had been on the job for six months; we were his first tourists. Thirty guards, he told us, are hired during crane season to keep local villagers from poaching. We paid $15, plus a tip, for our excursion. Thanh—serious Thanh who seldom smiled—turned out to be our best birder. "Before the war I saw many birds, even near Saigon. But today! I didn't know we had such a place in Vietnam," he told me.

EIGHT DAYS later I was ushered into the New York City apartment of Mrs. Jackson Burke, a friend and patron of the International Crane Foundation. Still in pursuit of the story behind the Tram Chim Reserve, I had been lucky enough to catch George Archibald where he had temporarily alighted.

A puckish fellow in glasses who was suffering from a bad case of jet lag when I met him, Archibald has a rare talent for feeling equally at home in the Vietnamese hinterlands and in a magnificent Park Avenue apartment, as long as the conversation revolves around cranes. A silver coffee service and four abandoned demitasse cups on a drawing-room table let me know that I had pulled him away rather sooner than expected from a most convivial luncheon.

Archibald is a Canadian who grew up on a farm in Nova Scotia and now calls Baraboo, Wisconsin, home. "Everybody realized that I was a bit different," he sighed as he settled into a silk sofa. "My first memories in life are of following ducks around on my hands and knees." After completing his undergraduate work, he enrolled at Cornell University in 1968, where a kindred soul in the department of ecology proposed that he study cranes. The idea struck him like a revelation. "There were birds and there were cranes, like there were apes and men," he said with passion.

Cornell in the late '60s was a hotbed of radical foment, a center of the antiwar movement. "Oh, it was a *terrible* time," Archibald recalled with a visceral shudder. "I wasn't involved with any of it—Vietnam, the political scene, the drug scene.

I found it all very frightening. I just stayed with my birds on an abandoned mink farm the university let me use."

With Ron Sauey, a Cornell friend whose family had a farm in Baraboo, Archibald set up the International Crane Foundation (ICF) in 1972 and built a Noah's Ark—or more formally, a species bank—of rare cranes from around the world. The birds were housed in pens and compounds and bred by artificial insemination. By 1979 the ICF had attracted the attention of the Smithsonian Institution and had raised enough money from private sources to purchase its own tract of land in Baraboo near the Sauey place.

Today 205 acres (83 hectares) of Wisconsin farmland houses a permanent crane installation, and the ICF's annual budget of $1.5 million supports a full-time staff of twenty-two that flies to Iran, Russia, India, Pakistan, China, Japan, Thailand, Korea, Vietnam, and Cambodia in pursuit of the universally revered but often endangered crane.

In 1988 Archibald landed in Vietnam, with German ornithologists from the Brehm Fund for International Conservation of Birds, to help the sarus crane in the Plain of Reeds, in Dong Thap province—and as it happened, the painted stork, the greater adjutant, the Bengal florican, and the black-faced spoonbill, which made a reappearance after the crane habitat began to recover.

Symbolic to the Vietnamese of long life, wealth, and happiness, a leggy crane standing on the broad back of a turtle is a revered motif in Buddhist pagodas and temples. The real-life population of cranes in Dong Thap had been nearly destroyed during the war: Intent on denying the Vietcong their protective forest cover, the U.S. military command had cut huge drainage channels through the Plain of Reeds.

As the wetlands dried out, unnatural fires—ignited in part by napalm—denuded the landscape. Helicopters swooped down on the big birds for fun, bored GIs emptied their rifles at them in "mad minutes," and hungry villagers killed them for food. The dried marshland in the area of Tram Chim was spared chemical defoliation, but the parched earth turned abnormally acid.

Now the birds were up against fresh, peacetime dangers. A human population explosion was affecting the environment with new settlements and expanding rice agriculture; and the government was launching a reforestation program, planting melaleuca trees (a freshwater mangrove) for medicinal oils and timber for houses. "Well," Archibald said, "we thought part of that land would make a *wonderful* nature reserve."

Luckily for the cranes, the governor of Dong Thap province, a former Vietcong commander known by his pseudonym, Muoi Nhe, had been having similar thoughts. Vietnam's leading environmentalist, Professor Vo Quy of the University of Hanoi, an ornithologist by profession, was also vitally interested in the project.

"In many ways, the Vietnamese are ahead of us in understanding environmental issues," Jeb Barzen of the ICF, a former duck biologist, told me in a later interview. "They are much more linked to the land than we are."

Remembering the beautiful area of Tram Chim from his childhood, Muoi Nhe had done what he could to restore a portion to its former state. It wasn't feasible to plug the American-made drainage ditches that slashed across the Plain of Reeds, because they had become important waterways for the people, vital to the transportation of fertilizer, rice, and other produce in the recovering delta. But the former Vietcong commander could and did construct a network of dikes around Tram Chim to hold back the flood-waters from the ditches during the heavy inundations of the June-to-October rainy season. The dikes were in place by 1984, four years before the western scientists arrived.

When the team of international scientists completed their studies, they determined that more elaborate measures were needed to encourage returning wildlife. A protracted period of negotiations ensued. The Vietnamese were worried that the foreign scientists' strictly environmental concerns would interfere with the country's needs for fish, melaleuca, and rice. "Ecosystem management and habitat fragmentation were new concepts for them," Barzen said. "Why should they believe our science?" Muoi Nhe was invited to Baraboo to share the American experience in wetland management.

The two sides reached a consensus in 1991. "This feels like the end of the second Paris peace conference," one of the Vietnamese scientists joked. The John D. and Catherine T. MacArthur Foundation ponied up money for sluice gates to control the water level at Tram Chim and offered additional funds for a small supervisory staff. The Vietnamese constructed a sturdy field house and exhibition hall. Tram Chim is expected soon to be a national park. Eco-tourism (what I was doing) is to be encouraged.

"Tram Chim is perfect for migrating cranes during the dry season, when the water level is low," Archibald explained. "They walk around very sociably, ankle-deep in water, digging tuberous sedges from the mud. But during their breeding season they live in Cambodia in solitary pairs, where they eat different things—a lot of insects and small fish." Protecting cranes in Vietnam, he concluded, would have to focus on Cambodia as well. So it was on to Phnom Penh.

Delicate international negotiations were old hat to Archibald by this time. In the mid-'70s he had mounted a media campaign to warn the Japanese that the red-crowned crane on the island of Hokkaido was in danger of extinction from development of the wetlands for dairy farming. The Japanese have a tradition of honoring cranes. Cranes figure prominently in their art, in their origami. "It was rather adversarial," he said. "They had thought the cranes were mating in Siberia, so it wasn't their problem. Imagine, a foreigner telling them what to do!"

The next stop was Korea. "I knew that red-crowned cranes and white-naped cranes wintered in the demilitarized zone between North and South Korea," Archibald explained. "The DMZ was the only place in Korea where any natural habitat was left—the rest had been ransacked by development." He frowned. "Now that North and South Korea are getting a little friendlier, there's talk about putting factories in those valleys. If that happens, the cranes are done for."

In 1976 Archibald went to Russia, intent on saving the Siberian crane despite a glacial response from Moscow. The former Soviet Union also honored cranes in the abstract as a symbol of life, peace, and renewal, as anyone who saw the 1957 Russian movie *The Cranes Are Flying* will recall. In an intricate set of maneuvers, captive Siberian cranes were artificially inseminated in Baraboo and the resulting eggs were sent to Siberia. At a propitious moment, the chicks were released into the Kunovat Nature Reserve.

From Russia it was a great leap forward to China, which turned out to have more crane species than anywhere else:

red-crowned, white-naped, Siberian, hooded, Eurasian, demoiselle, black-necked, and sarus. "China didn't open to us until after the Cultural Revolution," Archibald wearily recounted. "From 1979 to 1988 I worked there two or three times a year. A huge investment of time, but very productive. They treasured cranes in China as metaphors of long life, but they didn't understand that cranes needed big marshes." Inspired by the ICF, the number of wetland reserves went form zero to 22.

In 1984, while he was scouting cranes in the Australian outback, Archibald learned via a hand-cranked telephone that he'd won a MacArthur grant, a five-year "genius" stipend. "I went back to the campfire," he said, "and all these aborigines were sitting around eating kangaroo. I wanted to tell somebody, but there was no way they were going to understand, so I just sat down with them and ate kangaroo."

Last year he rented a Cessna and flew over Tonle Sap, the great Cambodian lake that drains into the Mekong, where he saw hundreds of storks and pelicans and thousands of other birds. "Seventy-eight percent of Cambodia is still wild woods and swamps," he exulted. "They have more birds there than I ever saw in Thailand or Vietnam." He promptly invited some Cambodians to Baraboo. "If their political situation every becomes stable," he said, "they can take tourists to see the temples of Angkor *and* the birds. For the economy, that's hotels and meals and everything else."

The visionary in Archibald cannot be stopped. "Africa," he went on. "Our project for 1993. Africa has six kinds of cranes, about 200,000 square miles (500,000 square kilometers) of inland wetlands . . . it's a whole eco-system we're trying to save, for birds, fish, and people."

Pesky wars. Famine. Population growth. Development. And on the other side, cranes—and the fragile dream of reclaiming their natural habitat throughout the world. It is no wonder that Archibald has attracted a devoted following of patrons, or that he half-jokingly compares his work to the enormous scope of the United Nations.

"You really ought to come out to Baraboo," he said, exhausted.

THE FALL *of a* SPARROW

. . . .

(SANDRA STEINGRABER)

WHERE THEY LIVE

They arrive uninvited, poor relations with little to recommend them and no plans to leave. Their motto: this'll do. A hole or a crevice is fine for them. So are rafters, ivy, a streetlamp, a rain-gutter clip. In Kansas, they reside in the continuously bobbing heads of oil pumps. In Turkmenistan, they excavate loess banks. In the Arctic, they squat in railroad roundhouses. Found on six continents, they are the world's most widely distributed bird. Urban or rural is immaterial to them. Except for this: they are never found more than 430 yards (400 meters) from a human structure.

WHAT THE EVOLUTIONARY ECOLOGISTS SAY

They are obligate commensals of *Homo sapiens*. Meaning they cannot live without us. They are our avian shadows.

They are Ruth to our Naomi. *Wherever you go, there shall I follow. Your home shall be mine.* They have disembarked from our ships. They have traveled with us along the Trans-Amazonian Highway. In northern Finland, in South Africa, across all of Siberia and the Americas, in the Bahamas, the Azores, the Falklands, and Cape Verde, we cohabitate. No one recalls when the house sparrow gave up the habit of seasonal migration.

WHERE THEY CAME FROM

They did not arrive. They are as old as agriculture, having speciated at about the time we first threw seeds on the ground and settled down. Their fossils have been found in caves near Bethlehem in Palestine and atop Mount Carmel in Israel. It was *Passer domesticus biblicus* to which Jesus was referring when he asked, rhetorically, "Are not two sparrows sold for a farthing?" They are the species God's eye is on. They are believed to have spread to Europe in tandem with the horse. The answer is probably Iraq.

WHAT THEY EAT

Mostly cereal grain and weed seeds. *Preglossale* is the name of the bone embedded in their tongues for husking. Stomach-content studies show a strong preference for millet over fescue. Catholic in their tastes, they switch to insects during the breeding season. They find dinner in the grillwork of automobiles. They rob spider webs. In Australia, they flutter before the electronic sensors of automatic doors and thereby gain entry into supermarkets. In Hawai'i, they gather on hotel balconies and await the emergence of honeymooning couples at breakfast hours. In Norwegian winters, they forage in total darkness. They are known to consume baby mice. They dislike eating alone.

WHAT THEY SAY

Mostly *chirrup,* which the Germans hear as *tshlip* and the British as *phip.* Sonographs reveal other vocalizations not distinguishable to the human ear. Throughout the day, they gather in communal roosts and chatter, presumably about foraging routes.

THEIR CONTRIBUTIONS TO SCIENCE

Much of what we know about the effect of light-to-dark ratios on sexual maturation comes from experiments using house sparrows, which are not legally protected. For this, they have been hooded, blinded, caged in darkness, castrated, pinealectomized, and defeathered. *Passer domesticus* is the lab rat of the avian world.

THEIR WORLD-RENOWNED EXPERT

He is retired biologist Ted R. Anderson, a man you might wish for your own father. Gregarious, curious, easygoing, Anderson hoped to land a research position after graduate school. Instead, he found himself employed at a teaching college in the soy fields of Illinois. He stayed on, raised a family, and studied sparrows. His life's work is distilled into a 547-page monograph. Nine years in the writing, it brings together literature from all over the world, involves translations from the Russian, and contains elegantly drawn graphs accompanied by captions such as "Monthly Changes in the Mean Volume of the Left Testis of a House Sparrow in Iowa." The book's final paragraph is this: "As I watch live television news from Baghdad, Gaza, Jerusalem, or Kosovo and hear sparrows chirping in the background, I sometimes wonder what opinion, if any, the house sparrow has about the havoc wreaked by its human hosts."

THE MYSTERY OF THEIR BADGES

Males sport a black bib, or badge, that varies considerably in size among individuals. Why? Badge size does not predict dominance. It is not related to command of resources. It is not a function of size or health. Females show no preference for large- or small-badged males. If size matters to the house sparrow, it matters in ways not known to us.

THE MYSTERY OF THEIR WORLDWIDE DISAPPEARANCE

Like the honeybee, the house sparrow is experiencing unexplained, catastrophic population collapses, including here in the Americas, but especially among urban populations in Europe. Unlike honeybees, sparrows generate few headlines announcing their ongoing demise. In England and Ireland, the number of breeding pairs has declined by 30–50 percent over the past two decades, a loss of as many as seven million birds. In some urban areas, losses approach 99 percent. Says Anderson, "Not since the Irish Potato Famine...have the British Isles witnessed such a major population decline." A lowered survival rate among juveniles appears to be the problem. Newly emerging avian diseases? There is some evidence for this hypothesis from Europe. Global climate change? There is some evidence for this hypothesis from Israel. The sparrow is the new canary.

AUTOBIOGRAPHY WITH HOUSE SPARROW

The spring my mother's breast cancer returned, I found an injured sparrow on the concrete slab of the school bus stop. I took it home and fed it milk-soaked bits of bread. Eventually, it learned to fly—but never properly because its left leg jutted out at a right angle, so it would flutter around me in loopy circles. Finally, it died. I told my mother it had flown away.

In college, I studied ornithology. My English-major boyfriend, wanting to join me in the spirit of birding, called me to the window of our wretched apartment, excited about the wrens in the hedge. "Those are just house sparrows," I shrugged. "They're invasive. They take over bluebird boxes. They're everywhere."

I have begun searching for them in parking lots, around grain elevators and loading docks, among the landscaping at gas stations, along subway station stairwells, under freeway overpasses. Are these spaces more sparrowless than they used to be? Is there an inanimation among the dirt and dust where, formerly, dirt- and dust-colored inhabitants cocked their heads? Have I taken too little care of this?

On an unusually warm evening, I met a colleague in the courtyard of a downtown restaurant. We looked together at the latest breast cancer statistics. The ivy shivered with sparrows, and their incessant chirping made conversation difficult. An ashen feather fell into my wineglass.

I was happy, happy to receive it.

MARTHA'S STORY

. . . .

(CHRISTOPHER COKINOS)

THE CATERPILLARS invaded Cincinnati in 1872. Legions of them methodically munched the leaves of oak, beech, maple, chestnut, elm, sycamore, and hornbeam growing along graceful streets and rough trails. They devoured the leaves of trees shading steep hills and hollows above the "Queen City" beside the wide Ohio River. People worried: Would the trees be stripped bare, would the lovely forest be destroyed?

Wasting no time, Andrew Erkenbrecher, a businessman and civic leader, raised $5,000 to organize the Society for the Acclimatization of Birds, then waited—no doubt restlessly—as a fellow Society member scoured Europe for songbirds with a taste for bugs. Armin Tenner returned with a trans-Atlantic cargo of 1,000 birds, including nightingales, European Starlings, and House Sparrows. Most of them were freed in May 1873 to wage war on any swarms of caterpillars that remained or might appear again.

How many of these European songbirds survived—and how the caterpillars fared—are details unmentioned in the few accounts I've seen. Cincinnati still has trees, starlings and sparrows, even if it lacks nightingales.

A month after the bird releases, Erkenbrecher and others began to raise stock for a Cincinnati zoological garden. It opened to the public in 1875, second in America only to the Philadelphia Zoo, which had begun operation just months before. The remaining exotic birds that Erkenbrecher hadn't released in the anti-caterpillar campaign became part of the new Cincinnati Zoo, which also featured a tiger, an unruly elephant, and one blind hyena. It was not an auspicious collection. (Later, as the zoo achieved more prominence and a sense of flair, it exhibited the rare Whooping Crane, as well as a "village" of live Sioux Indians.)

Had it not been for the caterpillars, there might not have been a Cincinnati Zoo for years or decades to come. Had the Society for the Acclimatization of Birds not transformed itself into a zoo, the story of Martha, the world's last Passenger Pigeon, would have been vastly different. Probably she never would have been on public display in Cincinnati, where, for years, she was the zoo's most famous attraction. Perhaps some other Passenger Pigeon would have been celebrated, then largely forgotten, as the last representative of this astonishing species.

So we have remembered, fitfully and often inaccurately, the lonely, lovely Martha. Many visitors to the Smithsonian Institution in Washington, D.C., have seen her stuffed specimen on display there. Birders who know little of Passenger

Pigeons often know the name of Martha. But most of us know nothing of her life and death—and her strange life after death.

The history of Passenger Pigeons at the Cincinnati Zoo begins in 1874, when one Frank Louck, Esq., of St. Bernard, Ohio, donated two Passenger Pigeons to the nascent facility. Those birds may have seen a few wild pigeons feeding and roosting in nearby trees and may have watched the last flocks of their kin fly above Cincinnati in 1876.

A few years later another Passenger Pigeon would be born and be named for America's First Lady, Martha Washington. Sometime in 1902, 1900, 1897, 1896, 1895, 1894, 1889, 1888, 1887, 1886, or 1885, inside an egg, a blind, cramped, featherless female Passenger Pigeon tucked her bill between her body and a wing. Pecking with her bill at membrane and shell for several hours, she began to fracture the white egg that had kept her safe. The temporary egg tooth on her bill helped with the ordeal; it would vanish after she hatched out. Assisted by an extra muscle on the back of her neck, which soon would become vestigial, the chick finally broke off a tiny fleck of shell. A splinter of light touched her skin for the first time. She squirmed and pecked. The egg fractured into wide cracks, until the chick stretched her neck upward. Born into a caged life, Martha might have enjoyed a taste of wildness: the parent birds feeding her their rich pigeon milk.

The year of Martha's birth remains uncertain because the man who ran the zoo—Sol Stephan, an ex-circus elephant trainer—changed his stories. Stephan and his son, Joseph, both gave multiple versions of Martha's birth. Sometimes they claimed to have purchased Martha; often they said she had been born at the zoo. So convoluted is this history that different female Passenger Pigeons at the zoo may have been called Martha at different times. Faulty memory, bad recordkeeping and a desire for enhancing the zoo's reputation seem the most likely reasons for all the conflicting accounts. Perhaps the Stephans felt it was more compelling to claim that the world's last Passenger Pigeon had been born in the facility they supervised. Sol also may have been given differing accounts of Martha's origin by the keepers, who were more familiar with the zoo's birds on a day-to-day basis. Unfortunately, files that might have shed light on Martha's origins were destroyed by a 1963 fire in the zoo's administration building.

We do know that in 1878, the zoo purchased some pigeons at $2.50 per pair. Some of these birds are known to have bred. According to an annual report, two Passenger Pigeons were born at the zoo on June 26, 1889. Was *that* Martha's birthday?

We also know that in fall 1888, a Milwaukee pigeon breeder named David Whittaker either purchased from or was given by a Native American four Wisconsin Passenger Pigeons. These birds had been captured close to Lake Shawano, just northwest of Green Bay. One died and one escaped, but the remaining two successfully mated. (Whittaker kept his birds in an outdoor cage near his house on a hill above the Milwaukee River where, when storms approached, the pigeons sat beside each other on a perch, tucked their heads in, then soon spread tails, stretched wings and flew up against the cage, wanting to escape.) University of Chicago professor Charles Whitman bought seven Passenger Pigeons from Whittaker in the late 1890s. From Whitman's group, apparently, the Cincinnati Zoo obtained Martha—or a Martha—in 1902. (That same year two pigeons escaped from Whitman's Woods Hole aviary.) It's worth noting that Sol Stephan explicitly wrote in 1907 that the zoo's last female pigeon was received from Whitman in 1902.

Though she never flew free, Martha did cross the country in Professor Whitman's care, as he took his pigeons from Chicago to Woods Hole, Massachusetts, and back again on the New York Central Railroad, according to pigeon researcher and fancier Joseph Quinn. Whitman kept research aviaries in both locations. Today a handball court beside brick apartments occupies the space where Whitman's Woods Hole aviary once stood.

By early 1909, the birds owned by Whittaker and Whitman had died, and just three pigeons, including Martha, remained at the Cincinnati Zoo. Had Whitman known earlier that Passenger Pigeons became more robust after eating earthworms, his flock, he believed, would have persisted.

Desperate attempts to find other mates for the zoo's pigeons came too late. There had never been a cooperative effort to captive-breed the Cincinnati birds when Passenger Pigeons were alive at various aviaries. At one point, the zoo even had a group of 20 Passenger Pigeons, which, if bred with others owned by different facilities and aviculturists, might have increased genetic diversity just enough to have saved the species. Perhaps there just weren't enough birds left. Hybrids that had been produced by breeding Passenger Pigeons with separate species turned out to be sterile.

Then, on an unspecified day in April 1909, one of the zoo's two male birds died, leaving only Martha and George (named, obviously, for George Washington). The last known pair of Passenger Pigeons anywhere.

Of Martha's life in Cincinnati we know relatively little, at least as concerns the textures of her days and nights. We don't know how often a bird keeper placed a tray of grain or nuts or earthworms beside Martha in her cage. She lived a mostly sedentary existence and watched visitors watching her and George, as the birds called to each other a sound that writers translated as *see? see?* From time to time, the pigeons sidled along branches and perches—a mark of mating behavior—and occasionally constructed loose, twiggy nest in a tree confined within their cage.

George died on July 10, 1910. His body was not preserved because the plumage was in a "poor state," according to one naturalist. Martha was now alone. Probably she could not have missed George in what we'd call memory, though who can say? Certainly she lived in the insistent aloneness of each moment after George's death. Her eyes saw cages, concrete, seeds, passing flits of birds beyond. She saw none of her kind, and this may have been a kind of anxiety in a bird as intensely social as the Passenger Pigeon.

Joseph Stephan, son of zoo General Manager Sol, had sometimes ferried Passenger Pigeon eggs from the zoo to his home, letting domesticated pigeons warm them. When the eggs were ready to hatch, Joseph returned them to the rightful parents, who, he wrote, "mothered them O.K." Now he watched the only pigeon left. There must have been days when Joseph wondered how long Martha would last, days when he walked by the elegant Zoo Club restaurant with its wide wraparound porch and columns, just across from the Band Stand. Leaning against a tree, he might have watched the meanderings of swans and pelicans on the lake or the gondola ferrying a courting couple.

From time to time, Martha flirted and stretched her wings, missing the flight she never really had. Mostly she sat. She ate at feeding time and stared beyond the metal mesh.

By the time it became clear that Martha was the last Passenger Pigeon, people were taking notice. The rival New York Zoo desperately wanted Martha, but Stephan refused to sell her. She would stay in Cincinnati surrounded by hills where her ancestors had once flocked and where the first trapshooting club in the United States had originated, using live Passenger Pigeons as targets.

Martha attracted a bevy of visitors to her home in one of the seven stone pagoda-like aviaries—the Bird Run—nestled among shade trees across from the Monkey House, the Pheasant Yard and the Carnivora Building. Her aviary measured 18 feet by 20 feet (5 by 6 meters), and a metal "summer cage" about doubled her living space. The aviary's tin roof, shaped to look like tiles, were almost as red as Martha's eyes.

On the aviary, Sol Stephan placed a sign, now lost, which declared that Martha was the very last Passenger Pigeon. "There were many scoffers," Stephan recalled. People had a hard time believing the pigeons were gone, all but this one. Ornithologists and naturalists didn't scoff. They arrived from faraway cities on pilgrimages to see Martha. For the first time, a creature about to be extinct had become a celebrity, subject to a bleak, surreal fame.

As Martha grew older, she might have stepped or flown forward each time Joseph arrived. Perhaps she ate directly from his hand. But, otherwise, she stayed motionless, which irritated some of Martha's curious visitors. Joseph remembered that "on Sundays we would rope off the cage to keep the public from throwing sand at her to make her walk around..."

One newspaper reporter wrote that Martha "is to be seen in the open air cage opposite the entrance to the lion house. There will be no mistaking the bird, as its drooping wings, atremble with the palsy of extreme old age, and the white feathers in the tail, make [her] a conspicuous object." Martha steadily weakened over the years, so the bird keepers lowered her perch until, finally, she could only stand on the ground, literally dragging her long tail.

"When the bird started to mope and show other signs of approaching dissolution," Stephan remembers, "I felt personal grief." Not only had Stephan cared for Martha, he had witnessed wild pigeon flocks, the bloody business of market hunting and pigeons caged for a trapshooting contest. He understood what had led to her singular status, even if, because of the times in which Stephan lived, he and others had failed miserably to imagine how the birds could have been saved.

As Martha molted in the summer of 1914, Sol and his keepers collected her fallen feathers in a cigar box. They knew that whoever mounted Martha's body after she died would need to glue the feathers back on her skin.

"The days of the last passenger pigeon...are now numbered," an anonymous reporter for the *Cincinnati Enquirer* wrote on Tuesday, August 18, 1914. These words appeared beneath Martha's picture:

It has lived for almost 30 years at the Cincinnati Zoological Garden under the tenderest care of General Manager Sol A. Stephan, but he has abandoned hope of keeping it alive more than a few weeks longer at the very most. That it has been failing rapidly has been noted for some time, but it was not considered more than the feebleness of extreme old age until yesterday morning, when Superintendent Stephan discovered it early in the morning lying on its back apparently dead. A few small grains of sand tossed upon it shocked it into activity again, and last night it was acting stronger and fed heartily when the evening feed was offered.

The article went on to explore the cause of this impending extinction, including the "wholesale destruction" of Martha's ancestors by market hunters, as well as the conjectured possibilities of sudden diseases and accidental mass drownings.

Sol Stephan awoke on the late-summer days of 1914 wondering each morning if Martha had made it through the night. On Tuesday, September 1, 1914, Martha roused from a warm night's sleep; the early morning low had reached just 72 degrees Fahrenheit (22 degrees Celsius). History does not record the name of her first human visitor. But the *Cincinnati Enquirer* for that day does record news of the Great War in black headlines of portent and carnage. A small poem on page 4 exclaimed, "All hail September. Hear our praise / Oh, month just newly born!" On the bottom of the same page ran a news item concerning an upcoming meeting in Winnipeg of American and Canadian lumbermen. By

1914, logging—implicated in the extinctions of the Carolina Parakeet, the Passenger Pigeon and the Ivory-billed
Woodpecker—had become a big enough business that its
practitioners organized conventions.

Tuesday's advertisements caught the attention of read-
ers: From 2:30 to 8:15, Weber and his Band would play
dance music at the Zoo Clubhouse porch; at Rollman
and Sons, the new fall hats had arrived, including those
decorated with the feathers of birds; and the New Arling-
ton Hotel promoted itself as an "attractive summer resort
[with] . . . Universal relief from hay fever." The hotel, coincidentally, was located in Petoskey, Michigan, near the site of
the last great pigeon nesting in 1878, where H.B. Roney and
his comrades had tried to bring attention to the illegal and
devastating slaughters there.

On Tuesday, September 1, 1914, travelers left Cincinnati
for other locales via the river boats *Chilo*, *Greendale*, *Green-
land* and the *City of Cincinnati*, all plying the mighty Ohio
River. A world away, the Turkish Army mobilized in support of the Huns. Just a few counties distant, in Waverly,
Ohio, near where the last wild Passenger Pigeon had been
shot 14 years before, a new school superintendent pondered
the semester's impending work. And later that afternoon,
under partly cloudy skies, the Cincinnati Reds would host
the Chicago Cubs, losing to the visiting team 8–7. All the
players would be drenched in sweat, the humidity reaching
74 percent, the temperature rising to 89 degrees Fahrenheit
(32 degrees Celsius).

While we have a record of all these details, the particu-
lars of Martha's death remain indeterminate and conflicting.
Martha died alone, probably at or about 1 PM on Tuesday,

September 1, 1914, as recorded by Schorger. This is the time and date now generally accepted. Yet, according to Joseph Stephan, "Martha died at 5 PM September 1, 1914. My father... and myself were with her at her death..." According to the *Cincinnati Times-Star* and *Field & Stream,* Martha "was found dead shortly after noon by William Bruntz, its keeper, beside [her] low roost..." Sol Stephan wrote to a Pennsylvania taxidermist not long after Martha's death and said that she had died at 2 PM on August 29, but nothing else support this assertion. Everyone agrees that the image of Martha taking her last breath while surrounded by stunned and grief-stricken ornithologists is just a fanciful legend.

Whoever first found Martha probably tossed grains of seed or sand or gravel onto her ragged feathers, hoping she'd awaken. She didn't, and thus the titanic vanishing of the Passenger Pigeon concluded, finally, on the bottom of a cage in the middle of a city busy with commerce and worry about war.

Eugene Swope, the Ohio representative of the National Audubon Societies, telegraphed Audubon leader T. Gilbert Pearson to tell him what had happened, provoking Pearson to comment—in the words of one newspaper—that Martha's death "is a calamity of as great importance in the eyes of naturalists as the death of a kaiser to Germans throughout the world."

Sometime on September 1, an anonymous writer at the *Cincinnati Enquirer* typed the obituary, reporting Martha's age at 29 and noting that:

> There will be no funeral for Martha. Instead, her remains, together with the feathers that she has shed

in molting, will be shipped to Washington, to be preserved in the Smithsonian Institution. Martha will
remain to be shown to posterity, not as an old bird with
most of her plumage gone, as she now is, but as the
queenly young passenger pigeon that delighted thousands of bird and nature lovers at the Zoo during the
past 20 years.

To keep the body from rotting in the heat as it traveled by train from Cincinnati to Washington, D.C., Joseph
Stephan "took her to the Cincinnati Ice Co. plant person-
ally," he wrote, "and supervised the placing of her body in a
tank of water, suspended by her two legs, and froze her body
in to a 300-lb. block of ice." Another version of the story has
Joseph Stephan cutting holes into existing ice blocks to hold
Martha's body. Pigeon fancier Joseph Quinn maintains that
Sol himself did the ice-cutting.

A photograph of Martha "on ice" raises some questions
about how her body was prepared. The picture probably
could not have been taken in Cincinnati if she had been
lowered into water and then frozen into place, unless the ice
was very clear. If the summer sun melted all the ice during
the long train trip, the photo could not have been taken at
the Smithsonian. The most likely scenario is that Joseph did
in fact take Martha to the Cincinnati Ice Company, where
she was slowly frozen in place, and that enough ice lasted
the journey to Washington for this photograph to have been
taken there.

A recital to have been presented at the Cincinnati Zoo
on the day that Martha died was to have included Francesco

Paolo Tosti's musical setting of George John Whyte-Melville's poem "Goodbye"—a grimly appropriate farewell.

> Hush, a voice from the far away.
> Listen and learn it seems to say.
> All tomorrows shall be as today.
> The cord is frayed, the cruse is dry.
> The link must break and the lamp must die.
> Goodbye to hope, goodbye, goodbye.

As the singer sang, the Stephans said their own farewells, whatever they were, to one of the most famous birds in the world.

.   .   .

ON THE morning of September 4, 1914, Dr. Charles Richmond, assistant curator of the Smithsonian's Division of Birds, called R.W. Shufeldt at his home. Richmond told Shufeldt, a physician, ornithologist, and museum associate in zoology, that officials wanted the respected naturalist to perform Martha's autopsy. Martha had arrived at midmorning, with the Smithsonian paying 54 cents for a delivery-due charge. An accession memorandum recorded the event, in Dr. Richmond's handwriting: "1 Passenger Pigeon *(Ectopistes migratorius)* in the flesh. The death of this individual marks the complete extinction of the genus and species..."

Shufeldt rushed to the museum and had the bird taken to a studio where he and Smithsonian photographer T.W. Smillie took a number of exposures. Although some tail feathers were missing and some feathers were soiled, most of Martha's plumage "was smooth and good." Martha, Shufeldt wrote, "had the appearance of a specimen in health..."

Then, at 1:15, Shufeldt and assistant taxidermist William Palmer left the museum, with Palmer carrying the bird. The men headed back to Shufeldt's house where Shufeldt could develop negatives and Palmer could "skin" the bird in a workroom. Throughout the afternoon, Shufeldt moved from the darkroom to Palmer's desk, taking more photos of Martha. They are gruesome pictures, images of exposed sinews and organs. Palmer placed Martha's brain and eyes in a jar of alcohol; by day's end all of her internal organs and tissue—minus skin and feathers—would be preserved in such a jar.

After a late lunch, Palmer left with Martha's skin and feathers. Once the Smithsonian's chief taxidermist, Nelson R. Wood, returned to town, he would mount Martha in a lifelike pose and the bird would go on display. Left alone with Martha's skinless body, Shufeldt lifted it and prodded. He looked carefully, discovering an inexplicable cut in the abdominal cavity as well as much damage to part of her liver and intestines; they were both disintegrated—"as though it had been done with some instrument." Further, many of Martha's organs were not where they were supposed to be, but Shufeldt offered no public speculation for the cause of this rearrangement. He picked up his scalpel and set to work, opening this or that chamber, finding atrophy in, for example, the ovary. The lungs looked dark; apparently, Martha had suffered recently from lung congestion.

Reading Shufeldt's autopsy notes, one confronts the probing of both a body and a spirit. Meditating on how people would react to Martha's display at the museum, Shufeldt envisioned much interest but little expectation that it would serve to stave off extinctions yet to arrive. "In due course, the day will come when practically all of the world's avifauna will have become utterly extinct," he wrote. "Such a fate for it is coming to pass now, with far greater rapidity than most people realize." During the autopsy, Shufeldt made a decision based not on science but on sentiment. He "did not further dissect the heart, preferring to preserve it in its entirety. . . as the heart of the last 'Blue Pigeon' that the world will ever see alive."

.   .   .

MARTHA'S HEART stayed whole, and her status grew. And as years passed, more and more Americans who visited her at the Smithsonian understood that there were, in fact, no more Passenger Pigeons. The rumors and "sightings" of the early part of the century ceased. The unalterable fact of extinction—as a kind of abstraction—became clearer once one looked at Martha's stuffed body. So, inevitably Martha accrued a certain symbolic power: Martha represented the finality of extinction and the consequences of the failure to conserve our natural resources.

In 1939, for example, organizers of a sportsman's show in Cincinnati tried to get Martha returned for the twenty-fifth anniversary of her death. They wanted her mute body to testify to those broad lessons. (The Smithsonian refused to part, even briefly, with such a valuable specimen.) In 1942, the chief biologist for the Soil Conservation Service wrote to the Cincinnati Zoo, hoping to obtain newspaper clippings about Martha, because he saw an analogy between the decline of the Passenger Pigeon and the loss of topsoil; he

wanted to make the parallel clear in soil conservation materials for farmers. Martha's death was, and remains, a kind of
ready-made lesson, a parable for other possible conservation
tragedies. Ironically, this attention to generalities, to "mean-
ings" about Martha, also helped create subtle obstacles to
understanding *the details* of her life and her species.

Because she was a symbol, Martha was able to take
her first extended flight. She left Washington in 1966 to
travel to San Diego, where the San Diego Zoological Society Golden Jubilee Conservation Conference convened in
early October. Zoo officials there had told the Smithsonian
that they wanted "something comparable in a way... to the
display in this country of the Mona Lisa..." The Smithsonian's Division of Birds Assistant Curator George Watson
agreed to send Martha so long as she was covered by a
$5,000 insurance policy from Lloyd's of London and would
be displayed only in a low-light setting, to avoid damaging
the feathers.

Technician Ted Bober carefully prepared a box for the
specimen and took the bird to the airport. Remarking on
Martha's first flight, a reporter for the *Washington Evening
Star* joked, "There is a question as to whether she should be
listed as a passenger pigeon or a pigeon passenger." Curator
Watson wasn't interested in puns. So he specified that Martha should "sit on [a stewardess's] lap all the way." A news
photo shows "one of American [Airlines's] prettiest," Miss
Nancy Evers, "who struck up an immediate attachment for
her feathered friend." If Evers didn't keep Martha's 15-pound
(7-kilogram) box on her lap during the entire trip on September 19, 1966, she did keep guard over the specimen. And
so Martha traveled first class to the edge of the Pacific.

After the conference, she returned on October 18, five days *after* the insurance policy had expired. But Martha was safe. Rather than deposit her in storage—where, years before, she had been misplaced—technicians carefully put Martha back on display. Her curators believed that's where she would remain.

But the Smithsonian hadn't counted on a respected wild-life painter named John Ruthven, who, one day in 1973, got some upsetting news: The old "Bird Run" at the Cincinnati Zoo was to be destroyed. The seven graceful aviaries, among the first buildings at the zoo, were to be razed for much-needed renovations to the ape facilities. Even the aviary that had housed Martha and the world's last Carolina Parakeet, Incas, was slated for demolition. Ruthven found the prospect repellent.

Ruthven's love for birds and woods was colored by the fact that Martha had died just ten years before his birth. "I didn't get to see her, and I regretted that," Ruthven remembers. So when the zoo's director, Ed Maruska, told him it would cost $50,000 to move the aviary 50 feet (15 meters) in order to preserve it, Ruthven offered to do a print of Passenger Pigeons and donate funds from the sales to that very cause. He raised $40,000, but an anonymous donor suddenly paid for the building's relocation. The $40,000 from Ruthven's sales were applied to renovation and remodeling.

The artist's activism wasn't the only reason the zoo agreed to save the aviary, according to Maruska. He tells the story of the Zurich zoo director who traveled to Cincinnati sometime in the early 1970s, specifically to see where the last Passenger Pigeon had died. The professor expected at least a plaque. But there was nothing, no marker, no sign.

Maruska felt deeply embarrassed. Now, by saving the aviary, the zoo would be saving history. And, as Maruska says, the whole incident reinforced a feeling about another kind of saving: "We made a vow that we'd never let a species go extinct at the Zoo again."

Ruthven's effort culminated in his winning permission from the prominent Smithsonian ornithologist Alexander Wetmore to let Martha out of her glass case one more time. Martha would fly home to Cincinnati. Her display would be the center piece of a ceremony formally launching public fund-raising for the aviary renovation and for educational programs.

On a June day in 1974, staffers with the Smithsonian's Division of Birds again removed Martha from her Bird Hall display. Technician Phil Angle took pictures as Martha was placed carefully—still on her wooden branch—in a plastic bag that nestled amid Styrofoam peanuts in a simple, sturdy cardboard box.

Ruthven asked Betsy Nolan, his New York-based publicity agent, to escort Martha to Cincinnati. Handed the box labeled "Martha: The World's Last Passenger Pigeon" (with contents insured, as they had been for the San Diego trip). Nolan took the specimen to National Airport and presented two first-class tickets, one for her and one for Martha. When American Airlines Flight 275 became airborne a few minutes after noon on Thursday, June 27, 1974, Martha was back in the sky. The flight crew even announced her presence on the plane.

She arrived in Cincinnati at 1:15 PM on what the mayor and governor had designated as Passenger Pigeon Day. Betsy Nolan looked for her bags, which never arrived. But at least the World's Last Passenger Pigeon would not spend the weekend in the backroom of some airport's lost-luggage depot.

For the next three days, this "feathered conscience," as Ruthven called her, appeared on display from 9 AM to 6 PM at the zoo's Reptile House. Bill Mers and Richard Fluke, who had seen Martha when she was alive, looked at her now-diminished colors. They remembered her red eyes blinking, her neck curving down as she pecked at seed. Mers recalled the sign that told of the zoo's never-claimed reward for discovering a mate for Martha. Fluke, a former fur trapper, said he had taken up nature photography to help raise awareness about the plight of threatened species. After speeches in Martha's honor, visitors could pay their respects, then attend a show of "The Derbys and Their Affection-Trained Animals from Television and Movies."

When the weekend ended, Nolan took the specimen aboard American Airlines Flight 400, leaving Cincinnati on Monday, July 1, 1974, at 7:50 AM and arriving at National Airport at two minutes after 9. By the afternoon, officials had the World's Last Passenger Pigeon ensconced in her glass case. She would never again leave the air-conditioned Smithsonian.

In Cincinnati, the renovation of the aviary continued, with the help of nature writer George Laycock, the Langdon Club (a local naturalists' group) and other artists and citizens. Cincinnati sculptor Robert McNesky unveiled his bronze statue of a Passenger Pigeon in 1976; the statue today stands at the entrance to a little path that surrounds the aviary shrine. McNesky also carved the aviary's massive wooden doors with reliefs of images of other extinct and threatened birds. The renovated building, listed on the National Register of Historic Places, opened on September 1, 1977, with another ceremony. Again, 81-year-old Richard Fluke spoke. This time he cried.

Just a week after the dedication, a burglar broke into an exhibit case at the new Passenger Pigeon Memorial and grabbed a relic, 16-gauge shotgun that Ruthven had donated. The robber escaped, cut off the barrel and later robbed a taxi and grocery store. "The assailant loaded the gun with modern shells," Ruthven tells me, laughing. "If he had fired, it would have killed *him*." Fortunately, no one was hurt, the robber was prosecuted and the gun was recovered for public display.

. . .

ALL THESE stories were in my mind one late spring day, when I finally had the opportunity to visit the Passenger Pigeon Memorial. I tugged on those dark, heavy doors, but they would not open. So I strolled around the small aviary and fumed in disbelief: I had driven all the way from Kansas and, now, could not get in.

Half-jogging across the grounds, I reached the office of Jan Dietrich, the zoo's school services coordinator. Waiting for her to fetch the key, I kept my distance from "Telly the Bald Ibis," who, with a long and threatening beak, watched my moves with great interest. When I returned to the aviary and Jan unlocked the door, I stepped inside—triggering an alarm, painfully loud, that drove us back in an instant. No one could steal a gun from this facility, I thought, and Jan rushed to get another staffer while I stood far from the open door. The siren blared. What I had intended to be a pilgrimage had instead become a series of absurd misadventures. I sweated and waited, smiling a forced smile while zoo personnel drove by slowly, back and forth on golf carts, and eyed me much as had Telly the Bald Ibis.

Finally, someone swooshed up the walk and turned off the alarm. But when I stepped back into the building, I couldn't find a light switch. Appropriate, I thought. I'm in the dark in Martha's home. So, with a flashlight, I peered at shadowed displays—an alligator skin belt, a net that had once trapped live pigeons. I admired Audubon prints of the Carolina Parakeet and the Passenger Pigeon, as well as actual specimens of each. And here, yes, was John Ruthven's shotgun, its barrel filled, lest anyone think the weapon could work.

I tried to imagine Martha in her cage in that very place, but couldn't. Too flustered, I felt no epiphany. I stood a moment in the dark while Jan waited outside and then I stepped, blinking, into the sunlight that filtered through trees and shrubs surrounding the limestone building. House Sparrows flitted through leaves. When two boys walked up the path and saw the shrine, one of them said, "This is where Martha and Incas died." I smiled at that small moment of recognition—not so small, really—then decided to go.

. . . .

RECENTLY, AT the Smithsonian, Martha has been in temporary storage to accommodate a building renovation. Perhaps someone will clean her dingy feathers with mild soap and water before she is put back on public display.

But in addition to her static body on a shelf or behind glass, Martha has a different existence. She abides as a "3-D" image on the World Wide Web. (The website address is kept confidential, except for those who need to use it for actual research.) Having photographed Martha with sophisticated cameras that captured multiple views for a three-dimensional effect, the Smithsonian has made the famous pigeon available to scientists who otherwise might have had to touch the specimen. Even before a researcher decides to study an object—measure it with calipers, say, or take detailed notes on colors—he or she must lift it and scrutinize. Such an initial examination determines whether the item is worth closer study. It's also damaging. "Seventy percent of the wear and tear on objects comes from handling *before* someone even begins studying the piece," explains Carl Hansen, branch chief of the Smithsonian's Center for Scientific Imaging and Photography at the National Museum of Natural History.

Martha's one-of-a-kind status made her a logical choice as an initial "3-D" photograph on the Smithsonian website, which will soon feature a wide range of other artifacts for on-line study. "She is such a classic object in the collection," says Hansen. So classic, he stresses, so important, that only the Smithsonian taxidermist handled her during the photo session. "If we had dropped her," Hansen says, "she would have broken into a million pieces, like Humpty Dumpty. Now, we know where every feather on her goes."

SEEING SCARLET

· · · ·

(BARBARA KINGSOLVER)

written with STEVEN HOPP

PICTURE A scarlet macaw: a fierce, full three feet (one meter) of royal red feathers head to tail, a soldier's rainbow-colored epaulets, a skeptic's eye staring from a naked white face, a beak that takes no prisoners.

Now examine the background of your mental image; probably it's a zoo or a pet shop, metal bars and people chanting about Polly and crackers, maybe even pirates, and not a trace of the truth of this bird's natural life. How does it perch or forage or speak among its kind without the demeaning mannerisms of captivity? How does it look in flight against a blue sky? Few birds that inhabit the cultural imagination of Americans are so familiar and yet so poorly known.

As biologists who have increasingly turned our attention toward the preservation of biodiversity, we are both interested in and wary of animals as symbols. If we could name the passion that kept pushing us through Costa Rica in our rented jeep, on roads unfit for tourism or good sense, it would have been, maybe, macaw expiation. Some sort of penance for a lifetime of seeing this magnificent animal robbed of its grace. We wanted to get to know this bird on its own terms.

As we climbed into the Talamanca Highlands on a pitted, serpentine highway, the forest veiled the view ahead but always promised something around the next bend. We were two days south of San José, in a land where birds lived up to the extravagance of their names: purple-throated mountain gems, long-tailed silky flycatchers, scintillant hummingbirds. At dawn we'd witnessed the red-green fireworks of a resplendent quetzal as he burst from his nest cavity, trailing his tail-feather streamers. But no trace of scarlet yet, save for the scarlet-thighed dacnis (Yes, just his thighs—not his feet or lower legs). Having navigated through an eerie morning mist in an elfin cloud forest, we found ourselves at noon among apple orchards on slopes so steep as to make the trees seem flung there instead of planted. All of it was wondrous, but we'd not yet seen a footprint of the beast we'd come here tracking.

Then a bend in the road revealed a tiny adobe school, its bare-dirt yard buzzing with activity. The Escuela del Sol Feliz took us by surprise in such a remote place, though in Costa Rica, where children matter more than an army, the sturdiest shoes are made in small sizes, and every tiny hamlet has at least a one-room school. This one had turned its charges outdoors for the day in their white-and-navy uniforms, so the schoolyard seemed to wave with neat nautical flags. The children, holding tins of paint and standing on crates and boxes, were busy painting a mural on the school's stucco face: humpbacked but mostly four-legged cows loafing beneath round green trees festooned with round red apples, fantastic jungles dangling with monkeys and sloths. In the center, oversize and unmistakable, was a scarlet macaw. The children's portrait of their environment was a study in homeland, combining important features of both real and imaginary landscapes; while their macaw surely had more dignity than Long John Silver's, he was still a fantasy. All of these children had picked apples and driven their family cows across the road, and some may have seen the monkeys they depicted on their mural, but not one, probably, had ever laid eyes on a macaw.

Ara macao was once everywhere in Costa Rica—in the lowlands at least, on both the Pacific and Atlantic coasts— but in recent decades it has been pushed into a handful of isolated refuges as distant as legend from the School of the Happy Sun. Its celebrity in the school's mural cheered us because it seemed a kind of testimonial to its importance in the country's iconography, and to the sporadic but growing efforts to teach children here to take their natural heritage to heart. We'd come in search of both things: the scarlet macaw, and some manifestation of hope for its persistence in the wild.

. . .

OUR DESTINATION was Corcovado National Park, on the Osa Peninsula, where roughly a thousand scarlet macaws constitute the most viable Central American population of this globally endangered bird. The Osa is one of two large

Costa Rican peninsulas extending into the Pacific; both are biologically rich, with huge protected areas and sparse human settlements. Corcovado, about one-tenth the size of Long Island, is the richest preserve in a country known for biodiversity: Its bird count is nearly 400 species; its 140 mammals include all 6 species of cats and all 4 monkeys found in Central America. It boasts nearly twice as many tree species as the United States and Canada combined. The park was established by executive decree in 1975, but its boundaries weren't finalized until many years later, after its hundreds of unofficial residents could be relocated. Hardest to find were the gold prospectors—who had a talent for vanishing into the forest—and the remnant feral livestock, though the latter disappeared gradually with the help of jaguars.

For us, Corcovado would be the end of a road that was growing less navigable by the minute as we ventured farther out onto the peninsula. Our overnight destination was Bosque del Cabo, a private nature lodge at the peninsula's southern tip. Our guidebook promised that we'd cross seven small rivers on the way, but we didn't realize we'd have to do it without the benefit of bridges. At the bank of the first one we plunged right in with our jeep, fingers crossed, cheered on by a farmer in rubber boots who was leading his mule through the water ahead of us.

"This will be worth it," Steven insisted when we reached the slightly more treacherous-looking second river. There was no bridge in sight, and no evidence that one had ever existed, although a sign advised *Puente en mal estando*—"Bridge in a bad state." Yes indeed. The code of Costa Rican signs is a language of magnificently polite understatements;

earlier in the trip we had been informed by a notice posted on a trail leading up a live volcano, "Esteemed hiker, a person can sometimes be killed here by flying rocks."

Over the river safe and sound, with the Golfo Dulce a steady blue horizon on our left, we rattled on southward through small fincas under the gaze of zebu cattle, with their worldly wattles and huge, downcast ears. Between farms the road was shaded by unmanicured woodlots, oil-palm groves, and the startling monoculture of orchard-row forests planted for pulp. The dark little feathered forms of seedeaters and grassquits lined the top wires of the fences like intermittent commas in a run-on sentence. To give our jostled bones and jeep a break, we stopped often; any bird was a good enough excuse. A dark funnel cloud swirling above a field turned out to be a vast swarm of turkey- and black vultures. With our binoculars we scanned the vortex down to its primogenitor: a dead cow, offering itself up for direct recycling back into the food chain. Most of the peninsula's airborne scavengers, it seemed, had just arrived for dinner. Angling for position near the carcass, two king vultures flapped their regal black and white wings and rainbow-colored heads at each other. "Wow, amazing, gorgeous!" we muttered reverently, gawking through our binoculars, setting new highs in vulture admiration.

At dusk, with seven rivers behind us, we pulled into the mile-long (1.5 kilometer) driveway of Bosque del Cabo under a darkening canopy of rain forest. Although the road tunneled between steep, muddy shoulders, but we could smell the ocean beyond. Our headlight beam caught a crab in the road, dead center. We slid to a stop and scrambled out for a closer look at this palm-sized thing. A kid with a box of

Crayolas couldn't have done better: bright purple shell, red-orange legs, marigold-colored spots at the base of the eye stalks. We dubbed this beauty "resplendent scarlet-thighed crab" and nudged it out of the road, only to encounter more just like it almost immediately. Suddenly we were seriously outnumbered. Barbara surrendered all dignity and walked ahead of the jeep at a crouch, waving her arms, but as crab-herd she was fighting a losing battle against a mile-deep (1.5 kilometer) swarm. These land crabs migrate mysteriously in huge throngs between ocean and forest, and on this moonlit night they caught us in a pulsing sea of red that refused to part. They danced across the slick double track of their flattened fellows, left by other drivers ahead of us. In our many trips together we've rarely traveled a longer, slower *crunchier* mile than that one.

. . .

WE SLEPT that night in a thatched *palapa,* lulled by the deep heartbeat of the Pacific surf against the cliff below us. At first light we woke to the booming exchanges of howler monkeys roaring out their ritual "Here I am!" to position their groups for a morning of undisturbed foraging. We sat on our little porch watching a coatimundi poking his long snout into the pineapple patch. A group of chestnut-mandibled toucans sallied into a palm, bouncing among the fronds; no macaws, though we were in their range now. We walked out to meet this astonishing place, prepared for any-thing except the troop of spider monkeys that hurled sticks from the boughs and leaped down at us, hanging from their prehensile tails in a Yankee-go-home bungee-jumping display. Retreating toward our lodge, we heard a parrotfish squawk in the treetops that we recognized from pet shops. Was it a macaw?

"Si, guacamayos," we were assured by a gardener we found shaking his head over the raided pineapple patch. Yes, he'd been seeing macaws lately, he said, usually in pairs, *"Practicando a casare"*—"practicing to be married." This was April, the beginning of the nesting season. Following their species' courtship rituals, the macaw pairs would settle into tree cavities, always more than a hundred feet (thirty meters) off the ground, to lay and hatch their two-egg clutches. The young stay with the parents for up to two years, during which time the adults do no more nesting until after these young have dispersed. This combination of specialized habitat and slow reproduction makes macaws especially vulnerable to an assembly of threats. The ravages of aerial pesticide spraying have lately diminished, as banana companies have left the country or switched to oil-palm production, but deforestation remains a phenomenal peril. Of the macaws' original Costa Rican habitat, only 20 percent still stands, all of it now protected. In addition to the Osa population, some 330 birds survive in the Carara Biological Reserve to the north, and others survive in scattered pockets from southern Mexico into Amazonian Brazil.

Dire habitat loss has become the norm for tropical species, but macaws and parrots are further doomed by their own charm. Such beauty doesn't come cheap: A poacher who captures a young scarlet macaw can sell it into the pet trade for up to $400 U.S. (The fine for being caught is about $325.) Since 1990, when the nearby town of Golfito was allowed to reduce taxes on goods passing through its port, employment from the import trade has grown, and poaching has noticeably declined. Farther north, however, in the economically undeveloped Carara region, the activity is still ubiquitous. Many conservationists feel their best hope is to introduce alternative sources of income for the poachers while educating their children about the poaching's long-term trade-offs—which could include the extinction of a national emblem before they're old enough to be adept at climbing hundred-foot (thirty-meter) trees. During our trip we spoke with several educators whose programs are aimed specifically at developing a family conscience about stealing baby parrots and macaws from their nest holes. Reordering children's attitudes toward threatened species may eventually influence their families, so the thinking goes, even within a culture that has traditionally allowed these birds to be harvested with no more moral qualms than a hungry coatimundi brings to a pineapple patch.

An organization named Zoo Ave goes a step further, by rehabilitating birds recovered from poachers or from captivity and reintroducing them into the wild. So far the group has released nineteen birds into the forest on the eastern shore of Golfo Dulce, far enough from Corcovado that the populations should remain genetically distinct. Of these birds, eleven are known to have survived. Zoo Ave's goal is to establish a population of a dozen or so breeding pairs in the area near Rainbow Lodge, adjacent to the newly protected Piedras Blancas National Park. Given that the total number of breeding macaw pairs in Central America is probably less than a hundred, every new nest cavity lined and filled with two white eggs a cause for celebration.

"El que quiera azul celeste, que le cueste," the Costa Ricans say—"If you want the blue sky, the price is high." The mix

of hope and fatalism in this *dicho* speaks perfectly of the macaw's fierce love of freedom and touching vulnerability. We stood on the cliff near our *palapa* above the ocean, scanning, hoping for a glimpse of scarlet that wasn't there. Today we would complete our pilgrimage to Corcovado, where we would see them flying against the blue sky, or we would not. On a trip like this, you revise your hopes: If we saw even one free bird, we decided, that would be enough. We prepared to push on to the road's end at Carate, gateway to the Corcovado forest, home to the country's last great breeding population of scarlet macaws.

· · ·

CARATE, ALTHOUGH it appears on the map, is not a town; it's a building. Mayor Morales's ramshackle *pulperia* serves the southwestern quadrant of the peninsula as the area's singular hub of commerce: He'll arrange delivery-truck passage back out to Puerto Jimenez, buy gold you've mined, watch your vehicle for a small fee while you hike, or simply offer a theoretical rest room among the trees out back. Indoors, suspended by wires from the ceiling, is a dazzling assortment of bottles, driftwood, birds' nests, car parts, and other miscellany—the very definition of "flotsam and jetsam," provided you can tell what floated in and what was jettisoned. Above the main counter dangles the crown jewel of the collection: a mammalian vertebra of a size generally seen only in museums. Under this Damocles bone we purchased a soda and plotted our strategy for finding macaws. Outside on benches under a tree, we learned from the *pulperia* regulars that Corcovado did not exactly offer the user-friendliness we were accustomed to in a national park. There are no roads in, no hiking trails, no wooden signboard maps declaring that "you are here." How do we get in? we asked. You walk, and watch out for snakes, we were told. It's a thick jungle; where's the best walking? On the beach.

While we chatted, a pet spider monkey sidled up to Barbara on her bench. Steven focused the camera. Nearby, a barefoot girl nearby watched intently.

"Is he friendly?" Barbara asked in Spanish.

The girl grinned broadly. *"Muerde."*—"He bites."

Steven snapped the photo we now call "Interspecific Primate Grimace."

.   .   .

THE STEEP gray beach offered rugged access to the park. The surf pounded hard on our left as we hiked, and to our right the wall of jungle rose sharply up a rocky slope. A series of streams poured down the rocks from the jungle into the Pacific. At the forest's edge the towering trees were branchless trunks for their lower hundred feet (thirty meters) or so. We began to hear, from this sparse, lofty canopy, the sound of macaws—not the loud, familiar croak but a low, conversational grumbling among small foraging groups. We jockeyed for a view, catching glimpses of monkeylike movement as the birds clambered around pulling fruit from the clusters at the tips of branches. Macaws are seed predators, given to cracking the hearts of fruit seeds or nuts. High above the ground is where you'll see them, only and always, if you don't want a cage for a backdrop. Both the scarlet and the other Costa Rican macaw, the great green, require large tracts of mature trees for foraging, roosting, and nesting.

It's hard to believe anything so large and red could hide so well in foliage, backlit by the tropical sky, but these birds did. We squinted, wondering if this was it—the view we'd been waiting for. Suddenly a pair launched like rockets into the air. With powerful, rapid wingbeats and tail feathers splayed like fingers they swooped into a neighboring tree and disappeared uncannily against the branches. We waited. Soon another pair, then groups of threes and fives, began trading places from tree to tree. Their white masks and scarlet shoulders flashed in the sun. A grand game of musical trees seemed to be in progress as we walked up the beach counting birds that dived between trees.

All afternoon we walked crook-necked and openmouthed in awe. If these creatures are doomed, they don't act that way. *El que quiera azul celeste, que le cueste,* but who could buy or possess such avian magnificence against the blue sky? We stopped counting at fifty. We'd have settled for just one—that was what we thought we had come for—but we stayed through the change of tide and nearly till sunset because of the way they perched and foraged and spoke among themselves, without a care for a human's expectation. What held us there was the show of pure, defiant survival: this audacious thing with feathers, this hope.

THE SPARROW'S FALL

· · · ·

(TREVOR HERRIOT)

SOME TIME just before dawn this morning, I was awoken by coyotes. They were making weird tremolo calls that sounded like loons, and by the time I figured out it was coyotes I was fully awake.

Then I realized that the harmonica-porch was silent. The wind had fallen. After two days and nights of wind it was dead calm. I'd been waiting for a windless morning to take my bicycle out onto the community pasture. I'm not much of a cyclist, but I brought one of our old clunkers out to the cabin, thinking it might allow me to explore farther out onto the grassland south of our property. On foot, I can only get so far in a morning before the birdsong fades in the heat of the sun, and it is time to head back. I'd never reached the middle of the pipit fields, and I thought a bike might get me there.

Unable to sleep anyway, I jumped into some shorts, put my binoculars around my neck, and headed out the door at 5:10, carrying some fruit, trail mix, and a bottle of water. I took one last look at the map we keep in the machine shed, planned a route, and straddled my bike. It is a bare-bones mountain bike that needs a tune-up and has never been off the pavement. Not really suited to off-roading, but neither are my legs, so we make a good match. My drumsticks are less than Grade A, but I thought a long ride up and down prairie hills might be just the kind of workout they needed.

Later in the morning, as I began rationing my food and water and fantasizing about a helicopter rescue, I realized I'd overdone it, gone too far into the pasture. On the return trip, I got to see some new places since I couldn't find the cow trail that got me there, and along the way I dispelled the quicksand myth that local farmers have been propagating. Not that there aren't some hellacious mudholes that will hold you down for a good spell. The myth I was able to disprove is the one that says you should never panic in quicksand because you'll get stuck worse than ever. Quite the contrary, I found that arm-flailing, wide-eyed panic, even with a bike overhead and no bottom underfoot, served me well enough.

I rode back the last half mile (eight hundred meters) uphill, pedaling hard in case Karen was watching from the porch. As I rounded the bend into the yard, my thighs screaming, I decided I should try a fancy dismount to punctuate my triumphant return as extreme prairie biker. Coasting to the front of the cabin, I swung off the bike and stuck a flawless Olga Korbut landing. The spasms locked onto my legs the moment my heels hit the ground. I think double charley horse is the technical term. My knees would not bend, so I fell over and rolled on the gravel a couple times to see if that would help, and that was how Karen found me: covered in mud and cramped from the hips down, writhing and yelling beside my fallen bike.

PEOPLE WHO live on prairie farms and pay attention to birds don't go for 5 AM bike tours with binoculars dangling from their necks. They don't wear Tilley hats and Rockports. They don't talk about rarities and compare life lists. They are a dead loss to ecotourism, never go on field trips because they live in the field already. They just notice things—walking to the quonset, sitting on the tractor seat, driving into town. And the drama they see in the comings and goings of birds, their annual striving to bring something to life in the land, runs parallel to their own work raising crops, livestock, and children.

What's more, a few of them manage to communicate with the birds. Some with gestures and kindness; some with words. Every family has a story about a grandfather or aunt who taught a crow to count or a magpie to speak; about dad feeding partridge in the yard during a storm; breaking the crust on a snowbank to let the snow buntings out; moving the horned lark nest from the furrow; leaving grass on the road allowance for the meadowlarks and sparrows.

These are the folks who bring to mind Wallace Stegner's famous lines about prairie dwellers: "It is a country to breed mystical people... perhaps poetic people... It was not prairie dwellers who invented the indifferent universe or impotent man. Puny you may feel there, and vulnerable, but not unnoticed. This is a land to mark the sparrow's fall."

With people noticing the sparrows and the sparrows sometimes noticing the people, a kind of mutuality between the human and the other-than-human becomes possible. If prairie people consider the birds more than city dwellers or people who live near mountains or forests, it's because they experience more of that vulnerability beneath skies that bring both blessed rain and deluge, zephyr and plough wind, sun and drought, snow cover and blizzard.

SOMETIMES WHEN they notice the birds, I hear about it, either on the air during "Birdline," or at home by phone or letter.

.   .   .

A phone call from a man with prairie chickens in his flower bed
His voice cracks in places, can't quite contain the mix of enthusiasm and concern. The message says his name is Lloyd and he has a question about prairie chickens—sharp-tailed grouse, that is. He's got a mother prairie chicken nesting in his flower bed. One of the chicks is out by itself and the mother is ignoring it. He wants to do the right thing but isn't sure what that is. Do they catch it and put it in a box to protect it, or do they just let it fend for itself?

.   .   .

A ninety-two-year-old man from Central
Butte writes about the birds of Last Mountain
A handwritten letter: small, round, and neat cursive on unlined stationery. The address is Central Butte and it is signed, "Yours truly, Edgar." There's a picture enclosed—an overexposed shot of a brown thrasher standing on a stairway

where seeds are strewn. You can see the frame of the window through which it was taken. After asking for help in identifying the bird in the photo, he says that he started watching birds in 1923 at the age of nine when his family moved to Last Mountain—a bird paradise. In the spring of '24 a farmer gave him a dollar for driving his four horses on the harrow for a day. He took that dollar and bought Taverner's *Birds of Western Canada*. After that he and his brother collected a single egg from thirty-seven different species.

In the fall of '26 he got to know some chickadees on the property. One was cheekier than the rest, brave enough to come to his outstretched hand and get bread crumbs. Within a week he had five chickadees all over his head and shoulders. They'd ride to the barn with him and in the morning when he went out to do chores he'd give a whistle, imitating their song, and they would come to greet him.

The birds disappeared for a spell, but the next fall he was out with a friend hunting rabbits and the friend said, "Edgar, there's a bird riding on your gun barrel." Edgar gave the whistle and four more chickadees came out of the bush to join the one on his rifle. He hadn't seen them for months and he was a half mile (eight hundred meters) away from the yard where he'd been feeding them, but they still knew Edgar, and responded to his call.

·   ·   ·

A man remembers the cliff swallows of Hafford
He heard the Hafford cliff swallows mentioned so he had to call in. They used to nest beneath the eaves of their buildings on the farm. You'd see ten or twelve of them working together on one mud nest until it was done. Then they'd get

started on the next one and the next until they had a bunch of them. Amazing to see them working together—like the original prairie socialists. Never had any trouble with bugs in the yard as long as the swallows were around. Some people didn't like the droppings they leave so they'd chase them off with guns. Then they'd be going out to buy a bug zapper soon after that. Hardly see swallows in the Hafford area since they put the power lines underground.

· · ·

A woman speaks to the bird with orange under its wings
She can't see very well anymore, but she can see that when it flies out of the nest hole there is a gorgeous flash of orange. She watches it through her bedroom window, an arm's length from the tree it nests in. She knows it is the mother, and she has been speaking to it every morning for several weeks. At first it was scared of her voice, but now it seems to like the sound. After her partner flies off for a bit, the mother comes out to listen for her voice. "Good morning, birdy," she says. "Sun's up. Good morning."

· · ·

A man from horizon who talked to larks and longspurs
He grew up on a mixed farm a few miles from a place called Horizon but it's not there anymore. That was in the forties and fifties. Ranched there himself until 1975 when his arms and shoulders gave out. Couldn't do the heavy ranch work anymore. Through the fifties and sixties he had two shelters on the outskirts of the yard—one for the cows and one for the weaned calves. The horned larks usually would come back in the first week of February. If he didn't see them by

Groundhog Day he'd get worried. By late March they'd be scraping out a nest close to the cowshed. The hen would sit on the eggs even when there was a blizzard and somehow she never got covered—maybe the snow bounced off the wall of the shed or something. One little horned lark would let him stay right beside and talk to her. If the cattle came too close she'd rise up, spread her wings, and almost hiss at them. They'd jump and get out of the way. If something happened and the eggs didn't hatch, well, no matter, they would start all over again.

When he was young he hunted and trapped, but then he got to the stage where he didn't want to kill birds anymore. He just wanted to admire them. In a lot of ways they're more intelligent than people are—the way they learn to take care of one another. The way they learn to trust you. Eat right out of your hand, sing right over your head, stay on the nest and never move because they know you, your voice, your clothes.

Even as a boy he always paid attention to birds, couldn't hear a song without stopping to listen. His dad didn't approve, swore at him for wasting his time with birds. Sundays were the days he was free to walk the pasture and visit the birds. Along the south side there was a ridge, an outcrop of rocks that stretches all the way from Estevan to Maple Creek, and in some places it goes underground. Around the rock, there would be some grass growing here and there in between. That's where the longspurs were. Chestnut-collared. It was nothing at all in the spring of the year to find a dozen pair in a quarter-mile (400-meter) length of that outcrop and they'd nest right there between the rocks. They felt safe there because the cattle would not try to step among the rocks.

Once he found a nest he'd take careful note of where it was, and then he'd come back every day, talk to the birds a little bit, quietly. They'd get used to him till he could sit down within five feet (a meter and a half) of a longspur on the nest and she wouldn't get up. The male would come, a little bit concerned, and he'd sit on a rock and sing and sing and sing.

They get to know you if you talk in the same low tones all the time, say the same words over and over again. He'd talk to them for a while, and they just seemed to take it all in—fluff up their feathers and preen themselves and put on a show. That's how he talks to all the birds—still does even now.

He misses the music of the longspurs, the songflights of lark buntings, and the way the burrowing owls once flew in to land on fence posts near him. Other people own the land now, and he would like to go back sometime and see if there is any trace of burrowing owls where they used to be. He's afraid the grasshopper spray got rid of most of them, but he'd like to see if they're still there.

Nowadays he talks to the barn swallows in his shop, where he repairs farm equipment. For thirty years, since he and his wife moved to begin a grain farm farther north, barn swallows have been nesting in his workshop. For the last four or five years, there's been a male who comes in through the west window where a small pane is missing. In spring, before any swallows have arrived, he's had the shop door closed and been working at his bench when that male has arrived for the summer. It comes right in through the hole in the window. The bird goes right to its favorite perch on the stovepipe over the workbench and it begins to chatter at him. He answers back, "So you're back again for another year." Two or three days later, a female will come by, and the male shows her around the nesting spots. She is usually nervous for a while, but he gentles her down, and pretty soon she's almost as tame as he is. That bird will sit within ten feet (three meters) of him, even when he's pounding or grinding something or the air compressor is going. He does not care one little bit. But if a stranger comes and he doesn't like the stranger's voice, he will give an alarm cry and dive at him.

Another time he saw a male swallow lose its partner when it had five flightless young still in the nest. The widowed male somehow communicated the situation to another pair of swallows nearby and the three adults together raised ten nestlings that summer, helping one another out at the two nests.

If the birds disappeared he'd miss their friendship. They are true friends, he always says. Human beings you can trust to a point; birds you can always trust. They're always going to be the same. If they like you and think they're your friend, they'll keep showing it until the day they die.

IN THE middle of my extreme biking safari, and before the exhaustion, the mud, and the double charley horse, I did manage to get to the center of the pipit fields. It was late summer and the pasture was quiet. A couple of vesper sparrows flitted here and there. Two mule deer bucks grazed in higher grass, their velveted antlers glowing with the tawny light of morning. I sat down to eat my apple and orange in a weedy field that had been "improved" by scarifying or scratching the sod to a shallow depth and then seeding it with alfalfa and crested wheat grass. Both are introduced species, but the wheat grass is a pernicious invader that contributes to grassland bird decline.

I remembered a biologist telling me that when you scarify and reseed a pasture to wheat grass, the food for birds decreases dramatically. Early-season grasshoppers, he said, are important for longspurs and Sprague's pipits in particular, but he has collected data that show these insects virtually disappearing from pastures improved with crested wheat grass. The brown-spotted range grasshopper, known to be important for songbird nestling survival, is abundant on unimproved pasture but next to impossible to locate wherever crested wheat grass has been introduced.

I looked on the ground underneath the introduced grasses and found the hidden disfiguration of pasture "improvement." A vital layer of life was entirely gone. On healthy native grassland, below and between the taller vegetation, a richly textured understory forms a dense pelt of ground lichens, algae, fungi, and club mosses. This "cryptogamic" layer is a galaxy unto itself, delicate and spangled with the bright growth of things that hug the earth. Any improvement that breaks the living crust will destroy it. Grassland biologists don't know what losing the cryptogamic understory will do to native grassland, its soils, plant, and animal ecology, over the long term, but one thing is known: once it is gone, it is all but impossible to restore. Grasses and forbs can be seeded, but the cryptogamic layer is too complex a mystery for artificial propagation to duplicate.

There is something so disheartening in the simplified pattern of disturbed pasture. The texture is close enough to real grassland to remind you of what is missing, and so it seems almost worse than the obliterating monotony of a grain field. It always makes me think of the choice someone made, and of the power of one machine-wielding person to alter permanently an ecosystem that has stood for thousands of years.

Ironically, though, having some non-native grass allows ranchers to protect their native range from being damaged by grazing too early in spring. The most beaten-down and weedy native pastures in our valley are those where the farmer merely releases his cattle into the pasture in May and then takes them out again in October. Range-management theory for northern grassland maintains that it is better to delay putting livestock on native grass for several weeks in spring because the natives are slow to get started and vulnerable to overgrazing during that phase. That means that most ranchers—as opposed to farmers who keep cattle—will have some land where they grow non-native grass that greens up quickly after snowmelt and provides feed during periods when their native range is being rested.

But the land I was on is not the private property of a single rancher; it is a provincially owned community pasture where local stockmen are allowed to graze their animals in summer. It may not have the federal funding of larger community pastures on the northern plains, but one would expect a certain amount of vision and stewardship even on a provincial pasture. Grassland biologists on both sides of the international border would love to have governments mandate a no-exceptions policy against breaking and scarifying any more native grass on government-owned pasture, including the millions of acres of leased land. Unfortunately,

the myth of the independent cowboy entitled to graze public land without government interference still holds enough
power to keep such common sense at bay.

I stood and strained to listen for distant birdsong, but
there were no birds moving or singing, aside from a family
of magpies yakking to one another in a distant bluff, and
two Swainson's hawks sitting on a large stone pile a mile (1.5
kilometers) to the southeast. The horizon was dominated by
evidence of the ultimate improvement for land classified as
unproductive: gravel quarries. A mile-long (1.5 kilometer)
ridge of stockpiled gravel loomed over the east side of the
pipit fields.

A jet passed by in a sky without song. This is what it will
be like, I thought, when the last birds disappear from this
pasture. In my lifetime I could witness the mixed-grass prairie and its birds receding from here, like the tide going out
for the last time, a long, slow wave drawing back into a sea
that exists only in memory.

It would be so easy to give up on these birds, write them
off as the collateral damage of our civilization's blitzkrieg
advance. Each spring I am amazed that the birds themselves have not given up. They come back, set up on a patch
of grassland, sing, court, build nests, lay eggs—even if the
grass is all wrong, the grasshoppers are scarce, and there isn't
the right kind of cover to protect nestlings from predators.
They fail, re-nest, fail again, then leave for the winter.

I sat in the cricket-song quiet for a good spell before a
bird finally spoke up. The softest, fading trill floated upward
from the pasture, letting me know that there was still at
least one Baird's sparrow remaining in the grass. How did it
fare this year? The breeding season was all but over and its

song was a faint shadow of its spring exultation, but it was unmistakably that of a Baird's. *Next year, next year. There is always next year.*

Farmers call this "next-year country" because they have the same tenacity—never giving up no matter how bad things get. For the birds it is more than tenacity, though. It is survival by passing on traits that until recently have allowed them to thrive in this particular place. We see it as fidelity, an unwarranted faithfulness not necessarily to one patch of land but to a matrix of soil, vegetation, and climate, to a life on the land.

The summer-ending song of a bird that very likely failed to raise any young this year cries out to a more perfect fidelity dwelling in this land that marks the sparrow's fall. In the gospel of Stegner's allusion, Jesus tells the peasants of Galilee that not a single sparrow falls to the ground without God's knowing and caring. Our ancestors came to this land with that gospel and many others consoling them as they stripped the prairie of its sod, and fought against drought, grasshoppers, and early frosts. The power of Stegner's adaptation is in the shift it makes from God to land. Not only God, but the *land* itself keeps watch, keeps faith—for in prairie we sense an abiding awareness and attention that may be more obscure in other landscapes. God knows the sparrow. The land knows the sparrow. The trick of remaining here is to become a people who know the sparrow too, who will not give up on creatures who ask only for a place in the grass.

CONTRIBUTORS

· · · ·

JENNIFER ACKERMAN is the author of *Sex Sleep Eat Drink Dream: A Day in the Life of Your Body, Chance in the House of Fate: A Natural History of Heredity, Notes from the Shore,* and the forthcoming *Ah-Choo! The Uncommon Life of Your Common Cold.* She also writes for *National Geographic* and many other publications. Her articles and essays have been included in several anthologies, among them *Best American Science Writing, The Nature Reader,* and *Best Nature Writing.*

· · ·

JOHN ALCOCK is a behavioral ecologist and emeritus professor in the School of Life Sciences at Arizona State University. He has written several books, including *The Kookaburras' Song: Exploring Animal Behavior in Australia, Sonoran Desert Summer, The Triumph of Sociobiology, Animal Behavior: An Evolutionary Approach, Sonoran Desert Spring,* and *In a Desert Garden: Love and Death Among the Insects.*

STEVE BRAUNIAS is an award-winning author, journalist, and editor in New Zealand. He has been editor of *Capital Times*, feature writer at *Metro* magazine, and deputy editor of the *NZ Listener*. He is currently senior writer and columnist with *The Sunday Star-Times*. Braunias is the author of four books including *Fish of the Week, Roosters I Have Known*, and *How to Watch A Bird*, which was selected as one of the best books of 2007 by *The Dominion Post*.

. . .

SUSAN BROWNMILLER is a feminist, journalist, author, and civil rights activist. She is best known for her pioneering work on the politics of rape in her 1975 book *Against Our Will: Men, Women, and Rape*, which the New York Public Library selected as one of the 100 most important books of the twentieth century. Her other books include *In Our Time: Memoir of a Revolution* and *Seeing Vietnam: Encounters of the Road and Heart*.

. . .

RICHARD CANNINGS is a consulting biologist who teaches field ecology at the University of British Columbia. He also works for Bird Studies Canada, coordinating Canadian Christmas Bird Counts, the eBird program, and the British Columbia-Yukon Nocturnal Owl Survey. Cannings is the author of *An Enchantment of Birds, Roadside Nature Tours through the Okanagan, The BC Roadside Naturalist*, and *The Rockies: A Natural History*; he is co-author of *British Columbia: A Natural History* and *The Birds of the Okanagan Valley*.

SUSAN CERULEAN is a writer, activist, and director of the Red Hills Writers Project in Tallahassee, Florida. She is the author of a nature memoir, *Tracking Desire: A Journey after Swallow-tailed Kites*, co-author of *Florida Wildlife Viewing Guide*, editor of *The Book of the Everglades*, and co-editor of *Between Two Rivers: Stories from the Red Hills to the Gulf*, *Guide to the Great Florida Birding Trail*, and *The Wild Heart of Florida*. Her essays have appeared in a variety of anthologies, magazines, and newspapers, including *Orion, Hope*, and *Defenders*.

. . .

CHRISTOPHER COKINOS teaches at Utah State University and is active in conservation issues as a member of the boards of the Bridgerland Audubon Society and HawkWatch International. He has written two books: *Hope Is the Thing with Feathers: A Personal Chronicle of Vanished Birds* and *The Fallen Sky: An Intimate History of Shooting Stars*. The winner of a Whiting Award, the Sigurd Olson Nature Writing Award, and the Glasgow Prize, his essays, poems, and reviews have appeared in *Orion*, the *Los Angeles Times, Poetry*, and *Science*.

. . .

DAVID GESSNER is the author of six books, including *Sick of Nature, The Prophet of Dry Hill, Soaring with Fidel*, and *Return of the Osprey*, which was chosen by the *Boston Globe* as one of the top ten nonfiction books of the year. "Learning to Surf" received the Burroughs Award for Best Natural History Essay. His work has appeared in *The New York Times Magazine*, the *Boston Globe, Outside, The Georgia*

Review, The Harvard Review, The Best American Nonrequired Reading, and *Orion*. He is currently an assistant professor at the University of North Carolina at Wilmington, where he edits the national literary journal *Ecotone*.

· · ·

CHARLES GRAEBER is a National Magazine Award-nominated writer and Contributing Editor for *Wired* and *National Geographic Adventure* magazines. His stories have appeared in *The New Yorker, New York Magazine, GQ, Vogue, Outside Magazine, Men's Journal, Ha'aretz, The M.I.T. Technology Review*, among others, and been anthologized in *The New Age of Adventure, The Best of 10 Years of National Geographic Adventure Writing, The Best American Crime Writing, The Best Technology Writing, The Best Business Stories*, and as Notable Stories in *The Best American Nature & Science Writing* and *Best American Travel Writing*.

· · ·

JOHN HAY, former professor of environmental studies at Dartmouth College and former president of the Cape Cod Museum of Natural History, is the author of sixteen natural history books, including *The Run, The Undiscovered Country, The Immortal Wilderness, In Defense of Nature*, and *The Great Beach*, which received the Burroughs Award. Peter Matthiessen called Hay "one of our very best essayists on the natural world."

· · ·

BERND HEINRICH is the author of numerous award-winning books, including *Winter World: The Ingenuity of Animal*

Survival, Mind of the Raven: Investigations and Adventures with Wolf-Birds, and *Why We Run: A Natural History,* and has received countless honors for his scientific work. He also writes for *Scientific American, Outside, American Scientist,* and *Audubon.* He is professor emeritus of biology at the University of Vermont and has made major contributions to the study of insect physiology and behavior, as well as bird behavior.

· · ·

TREVOR HERRIOT is an award-winning author, naturalist, and speaker. His first book, *River in a Dry Land,* won the Drainie-Taylor Biography Prize, the Saskatchewan Book of the Year Award, the Regina Book Award, a CBA Libris Award, and was shortlisted for the Governor General's Award. *Jacob's Wound* and *Grass, Sky, Song* were both shortlisted for the Writers' Trust Non-Fiction Prize. Herriot is active in the Nature Conservancy of Canada, is featured regularly on CBC Radio, and is a frequent guest on the call-in show *Blue Sky.*

· · ·

KENN KAUFMAN is the originator of the Kaufman Field Guide series, which includes books on birds, butterflies, mammals, and insects. He has also written *Lives of North American Birds, Kingbird Highway,* and the *Peterson Field Guide to Advanced Birding.* He is field editor for *Audubon* magazine and a regular contributor to numerous birding magazines. A devoted conservationist, he works vigorously to promote the appreciation and protection of nature.

DAN KOEPPEL, author of the critically acclaimed memoir *To See Every Bird on Earth* and of *Banana: The Fate of the Fruit That Changed the World*, is an award-winning outdoors and adventure writer whose work has been featured in *The New York Times Magazine, Outside, National Geographic Adventure*, the *Los Angeles Times*, and *Popular Science*. He also writes extensively in a variety of mountain biking periodicals.

. . .

BARBARA KINGSOLVER'S bestselling books of fiction, poetry, and creative non-fiction include the novels *The Bean Trees, Animal Dreams*, and *The Poisonwood Bible*. Translated into nineteen languages, her work has won a devoted worldwide readership and many awards, including the National Humanities Medal. Her most recent books are the highly praised, *New York Times* bestselling *Animal, Vegetable, Miracle*, and the novel *Lacuna*.

. . .

RICHARD MABEY is a naturalist, writer, and broadcaster with a special interest in the relationship between nature and culture. His books include *Food For Free, Country Matters*, and *Flora Britannica* as well as an award-winning biography of Gilbert White and his memoir, *Nature Cure*, which was shortlisted for the Whitbread and Ondaatje prizes. He has written a regular column for *BBC Wildlife* magazine, and has also written for *The Sunday Times, The Times, The Sunday Telegraph*, and the *Countryman*.

ELLEN MELOY'S books *Raven's Exile: A Season on the Green River* and *The Last Cheater's Waltz* earned many awards including the Utah Book Award and the Writer's Award from the Whiting Foundation. *The Anthropology of Turquoise: Meditations on Landscape, Art, and Spirit* was nominated for the Pulitzer Prize for non-fiction. Meloy's final book, *Eating Stone: Imagination and the Loss of the Wild*, was published in 2005, a year after her death.

· · ·

JIM MILLER teaches at the University of Illinois in the Department of Natural Resources and Environmental Sciences. Through his research, he attempts to advance an understanding of ways to accommodate the needs of native species in landscapes dominated by human activities, with the goal of protecting biodiversity. His work has been published in numerous academic and science journals, and in *Best American Nature Writing*.

· · ·

DAVID PITT-BROOKE writes for a variety of nature and wildlife publications. He was an Environmental Education Officer for Parks Canada for ten years, and has also bred falcons, collared caribou, and implanted radios in rattlesnakes. His first book was *Chasing Clayoquot: A Wilderness Almanac*. He is currently working on a book about his pilgrimage through the grasslands of central British Columbia. He received a Canadian Science Writers' Association Award for Outstanding Contribution to Science Journalism.

SANDRA STEINGRABER is an internationally recognized expert on the environmental links to cancer and reproductive health. She is the author of *Post-Diagnosis,* a volume of poetry, *Living Downstream: An Ecologist Looks at Cancer and the Environment,* and *Having Faith: An Ecologist's Journey to Motherhood.* Steingraber is Distinguished Visiting Scholar at Ithaca College in Ithaca, New York. The Sierra Club heralded Steingraber as "the new Rachel Carson," and in 2001 she received the Rachel Carson Leadership Award.

ACKNOWLEDGMENTS

. . . .

"Summer" excerpted from *How to Watch A Bird* by Steve Braunias (Wellington, NZ: Awa Press). Copyright © 2008 by Steve Braunias. Used by permission of Awa Press.

"Not Quite the West" excerpted from *Kingbird Highway: The Story of a Natural Obsession that Got A Little Out of Hand* by Kenn Kaufman (New York: Houghton Mifflin). Copyright © 1997 by Kenn Kaufman. Used by permission of Houghton Mifflin Harcourt Publishing Company.

"Western Meadowlark" excerpted from *An Enchantment of Birds: Memories from a Birder's Life* by Richard Cannings (Vancouver: Greystone Books). Copyright © 2007 by Richard Cannings. Used by permission of Greystone Books.

"Learning to Surf" by David Gessner first appeared in *Orion* Magazine, March/April 2006 (www.oriononline.org). Copyright © 2006 by David Gessner. Used by permission of the author.

"A Society of Muttonbirds" excerpted from *The Kookaburras' Song: Exploring Animal Behavior in Australia* by John Alcock (Tucson: University of Arizona Press). Copyright © 1988 by The Arizona Board of Regents. Used by permission of University of Arizona Press.